WITHDRAWN

INNER SANCTUM
BOOKS FOR VICTORY

MISSION TO MOSCOW
by Joseph E. Davies

VICTORY THROUGH AIR POWER
by Major Alexander P. de Seversky

THE INNER SANCTUM EDITION OF
WAR AND PEACE
by Leo Tolstoy

SHOOTING THE RUSSIAN WAR
by Margaret Bourke-White

HOW WAR CAME
by Forrest Davis and Ernest K. Lindley

REPORT ON ENGLAND
by Ralph Ingersoll

THIS IS LONDON
by Edward R. Murrow

ALL OUT
by Samuel Grafton

REPORT FROM TOKYO

A Message to the American People

By JOSEPH C. GREW

United States Ambassador to Japan, 1932 to 1941

19 — 42

Simon and Schuster

NEW YORK

Contents

PREFACE   vii

INTRODUCTORY NOTE   xi

PRESIDENT ROOSEVELT'S MESSAGE TO CONGRESS   xxv

1. RETURN FROM JAPAN   3

2. WHY WAR CAME   11

3. THE EXTENT OF THE JAPANESE CHALLENGE   19

4. HOW WE MUST FIGHT TO DEFEAT JAPAN   26

5. WHY WE CAN NO LONGER DO BUSINESS WITH JAPAN   37

6. JAPANESE YOUTH   50

7. TRUTH IN JAPAN   55

8. IS THIS A RACIAL WAR?   60

9. OUR ALLIES IN THE PACIFIC   67

10. JAPAN: THE PLEDGE AND THE PERFORMANCE   72

11. BUILDING THE FUTURE—A POSTSCRIPT   86

Preface

The purpose of this book is to overcome a fallacy in the thinking of a large proportion of my fellow countrymen about our war with Japan. That thinking, so far as I have been able to gauge it since my return from Tokyo on August 25, 1942, is clearly influenced by preconceived but unfounded assumptions as to Japan's comparative weakness and vulnerability in war. Such thinking is not only erroneous; it constitutes a grave danger to our fighting spirit, our war effort, and our united will to win. If persisted in, it will be a serious obstacle to our ultimate victory.

During my mission to Japan I kept our Government informed, especially throughout the year 1941, of the ever-present danger of an all-out, do-or-die attempt by the Japanese military machine to render their country, through vast territorial expansion, secure against economic pressures from abroad. I reported that Japan might strike "with dangerous and dramatic suddenness." This is precisely what happened at Pearl Harbor. The decision of our Government before then to construct a two-ocean Navy and to build up and strengthen our Army and Air Force were the outstanding measures, among many others, which prove beyond any shadow of doubt that the Administration was alive to that danger.

A primary axiom in war is to know your enemy. The American people, as a whole, are dangerously ill-informed regarding the strength of one of our enemies—Japan. I have lived in Japan for the past ten years; I know the Japanese people and I know a good deal about the Japanese military machine, its constant strengthening, its intensive training over many years, its piling up of reserves, its fighting spirit, and its overweening ambition first to conquer and wholly to control the area and people of Greater East Asia including the South Seas and, later, to conquer and wholly to control areas and peoples of other parts of the world, including our Western Hemisphere. Once in unchallenged control of those far-flung territories in Asia and the Pacific, with their wealth in raw materials and their almost unlimited resources in labor readily to be enslaved for the processing of those materials and for the intensive building of naval and commercial ships, the Japanese would, without question, directly threaten our own shores and our own homes. That threat might not seriously develop in a year, or two years, or even five years, but a Japan firmly in possession of and successfully exploiting the vast area which her armed forces have seized during the past twelve months would constitute for us as grave a menace as a Nazi Germany securely in control of the European continent would constitute for the British Isles. Even today we are face to face with a powerful, resourceful, utterly ruthless, and altogether dangerous enemy. We must defeat that enemy, conclusively, and leave no margin for a recurrence of that threat in future.

I have been trying to tell these things to our people in public addresses and broadcasts, of which there will be many still to come, but it seems to me desirable to assemble in this small book, for publication on a momentous anniversary, December 7, 1942, a few of those remarks. I hope they will be read by every American in every walk of life throughout our land. I hope they will be read, too, by other peoples of the United Nations. For only when all of us realize and appreciate the facts herein presented shall we be able to swing unanimously into line in supporting and

PREFACE

*furthering to the maximum extent of our several capacities the effort
required for winning the war.*

*This book is not directed against those erstwhile Japanese friends of
ours whom, during our long stay in their country, we admired, respected,
and loved. Though powerless to prevent the war, many of them worked
to avoid war and were deeply shocked when war came.*

*Let me close this brief preface with a quotation I have used in several
of my speeches—a quotation from the diary of an American soldier, Mar-
tin Treptow, written shortly before he died for his country at Château
Thierry in 1918, for those flaming words of his should constitute a guid-
ing torch that every red-blooded American should take up and carry with
proud determination to victory:*

*"I will work; I will save; I will sacrifice; I will endure; I will fight
cheerfully and do my utmost;* as if the whole struggle depended on me
alone."

Joseph C. Grew

*Washington, D. C.
November, 1942*

Introductory Note

In August, 1941, I received a letter from a Japanese friend, who wrote expressing the hope that the American Government would ultimately come to sympathize and, if possible, to co-operate with Japan in pursuing her "legitimate interests and aspirations."

I believe that my reply, which follows, may usefully serve as a background for the text of this small book. Copies of this reply were sent to a considerable number of important and influential Japanese both in and outside the Government.

EMBASSY OF THE

UNITED STATES OF AMERICA

Tokyo, September 1, 1941

My dear ———

I well know how deeply the present situation in international affairs is paining you, just as it is paining me.

It is a dark and critical period that we are passing through, but during the past nine years I have seen our two countries pass through several crises and surmount them, and I firmly believe that we shall eventually surmount the present one. I cannot visualize the utter stupidity of war ensuing between Japan and the United States, and if ever a break should occur I feel convinced that it will not come as a result of any deliberated act on the part of either of our Governments but rather through some

xi

unfortunate act brought about by extremist elements. I know very well that Prince Konoye and Admiral Toyoda, and the President and Mr. Hull, are doing their utmost to avoid war and are dealing with the situation with the highest statesmanship, courage, and farsighted vision. Pray God that they may be allowed to achieve success and that their enlightened efforts will not be wrecked by shortsighted and intransigent elements in either country.

But many things have been done over the past several years and are being done today which are not permitted to come to the knowledge of the public in Japan, and therefore it is very difficult—I should say impossible—for the Japanese people to view the situation objectively and to weigh all the factors which have led to the present unhappy pass in our relations. Merely as an illustration, I doubt if many Japanese know of the serious incidents which occurred only recently, when Japanese aviators attacked our Embassy and our Navy ship the *Tutuila,* sister ship of the ill-fated *Panay,* in Chungking on several occasions; our Embassy was damaged, fortunately without loss of American lives, and a bomb missed the *Tutuila* by only a few yards, but damaged her. Our Embassy and our ship are in a safety zone, recognized by the Japanese Government, and no military objectives are near them. Three American officers who witnessed the attack on the *Tutuila* from a near-by hill have officially expressed their opinion that the attack was deliberate or, at the very least, due to criminal negligence. The Japanese planes came over in perfectly clear weather; one plane left the others and took a course directly over the *Tutuila,* dropping its bomb as it passed over the ship and missing her only by a split second of time.

If the ship had been sunk, or if our Ambassador had been killed, as might easily have occurred, I do not think that the present status of our relations could have stood the strain because the entire American people would have become enflamed. I said this to Mr. Matsuoka early in June after the first attack on our Embassy, when the buildings had been actually hit; I said that never during my nine years in Japan had I been more anxious over any situation than these obviously deliberate attacks on our Embassy and ship, and that of all the difficult problems with which the Minister was faced, I felt certain that he was confronted with no more serious problem than this one. Mr. Matsuoka replied, "I agree with you," yet the attacks continued, three or four of them within a few weeks. By such hairbreadth escapes are America and Japan still hoping and working to avoid a break.

You write of the desirability of our recognizing Japan's legitimate interests and aspirations. Indeed our Government has time and time again, and only recently, expressed its full appreciation of Japan's legitimate interests and aspirations, realizing that Japan, restricted as she is in her islands, must have access to raw materials, markets for the products of her industries, and a free flow of trade and commerce. Nevertheless, unless Japan is willing to abandon aggression by force, there can be no hope for an improvement in our relations.

We know by sad and bitter practical experience that Japan's so-called "New Order in East Asia" and "Co-Prosperity Sphere" visualize no neighborly relations on the basis of reciprocity and a free give-and-take but rather an order in which Japanese interests, or what she conceives to be her interests, are to be predominant and to be exercised to the exclusion of the legitimate interests of other countries. We have watched the gradual but inexorable elimination of our own legitimate interests over these past several years, our long-standing and patiently established business, commercial, industrial, banking, and cultural interests, all legitimate and co-operative activities, progressively ousted first from Manchuria, and then, in turn, from North China, the ports, the Yangtze, and now they are in process of being excluded from Indo-China, in spite of the most categorical assurances and promises that the Open Door and equal opportunity would be scrupulously observed everywhere. Every Foreign Minister —especially Hirota, Arita, Nomura—has given us such promises, but not one of those promises has been carried out.

Why? Those promises were unquestionably given in good faith. But the military would not permit their implementation. Japanese armed force has prevented their implementation. Is it surprising that when Admiral Toyoda assures me of Japan's peaceful intentions, I am obliged to recount to him those past bitter experiences? How, in the light of those experiences, can my Government believe any such promise or assurance given us by any Japanese Government?

Highly placed Japanese are constantly talking and writing about Anglo-American imperialism in East Asia, about Anglo-American encirclement. Please look at the record. So far as the United States is concerned, we have always wished Japan well, have proved our friendship by concrete acts. In the old days we protected Japan from unequal treaties which other nations attempted to foist upon her. We counseled and actively helped Japan in her splendid efforts to become a great modern power. At the time of the Great Earthquake we did everything in our power, spiritually and materially, to show our friendship for Japan and to support and aid her in her hour of trial. Up until the invasion of Manchuria in 1931 we were negotiating with China for the abrogation of the unequal treaties, ready and willing to abandon our extraterritorial rights, including our extraterritorial judicial, commercial, and customs rights, and this would unquestionably have come to pass if Japan had not set out on her long course of aggression and the use of armed force as an instrument of national policy. . . .

I do not believe that you, my dear friend, or many of your friends, have any detailed knowledge of the patience and forbearance exercised by the American Government and people in the face of the truly outrageous treatment of our own legitimate interests at the hands of Japanese authorities, both military and civil, during these past years.

Our missions throughout China, including churches, hospitals, universities, and schools, have been ruthlessly bombed and wrecked and American missionaries and their families have been killed or injured in spite of the fact that such buildings were clearly marked by American flags both flying and painted on the roofs and their precise location marked on maps submitted to the Japanese military authorities, showing that they were seldom if ever in the neighborhood of any military objectives. There can be no shadow of doubt that these cruel and brutal attacks were planned and executed with careful intention. Accidents can happen, but not two or three hundred accidents of the same kind. It is a saying among the Chinese that when a Chinese city or town is bombed by Japanese aviators, the most dangerous spot and the one to get far away from is the American mission. It is perfectly clear that the Japanese bombers were following a concerted plan to drive American missionary, educational, medical, and cultural activities out of China permanently. We might have broken relations with Japan on this issue alone, but we didn't; we remained patient and, permit me to say, long-suffering. Yet you write: "Even an incident one tenth as bad as that of the bombing of Iran will never take place in this our part of the world."

The same concerted drive against our business firms, banks, industrial interests, commercial and shipping activities, has steadily and inexorably progressed, first in Manchuria, then in North China, the ports, the Yangtze valley, and now in Indo-China, where American-owned cargoes have been ruthlessly seized and shipped away. Is this the Open Door and equal opportunity, of the scrupulous safeguarding of which I so often received the most categorical assurances from successive Japanese governments?

Meanwhile the southward advance progressed step by step, one step at a time, first occupation, then consolidation, a pause to watch its result, and then another forward step. All this time many of your leading men, admirals, generals, retired ambassadors, prominent writers, publicists, and politicians, were contributing articles to the daily press and magazines advocating the rapid pushing of the southward advance and the elimination of the Americans and Europeans and all of their interests and activities from the entire sphere of "Greater East Asia including the South Seas." And this advance was to be pursued first by high-pressure diplomacy and then, if necessary, by force.

Can you possibly believe that if France had not been powerless she would have allowed the occupation of bases, both naval and aviation, in Indo-China? Or can you possibly believe that Great Britain, completely occupied as she is with the war in Europe, where her own national life and the safety of the British Isles are at stake, would or could start a program of unprovoked aggression and invasion against Indo-China or Thailand, or that the United States or the Netherlands would ever even consider such aggression? The fallacy of the alleged ABCD "encirclement" is too patent to fool even a schoolboy—if he knows the facts. But in the light of Japan's recent actions and the clear intentions of so many of Japan's prominent men as expressed by them in their articles in the daily newspapers and magazines, is it surprising that the ABCD powers realize beyond a shadow of a doubt that it is they who are being "encircled" and that Malaya, Burma, Singapore, the Netherlands East Indies, and the Philippines themselves are in direct line for future aggressive moves by Japan in establishing and consolidating the so-called "New Order in Greater East Asia including the South Seas" and that defensive measures had therefore to be taken?

From all that has passed and from all that is being said and written and done, the evidence is clear for all to see that what is euphemistically called the "Co-Prosperity Sphere" means eventual Japanese hegemony over all the areas therein contained. From all the evidence, is it not abundantly clear that we in the United States must now and in future be guided alone by facts and actions and that we can no longer rely on words or assurances of peaceful intentions? I have stated this fact categorically to Admiral Toyoda, after recounting to him our past bitter experiences when we did rely on such assurances.

To turn to the China affair. Few people know, but I know, that about ten days or a fortnight after the outbreak of hostilities in July, 1937, Chiang Kai-shek sent a message through the British Embassy here to the Japanese Government, offering an immediate armistice and the withdrawal of all Chinese troops if the Japanese troops would likewise withdraw to a given line pending negotiations. Mr. Dodds was then the British Chargé d'Affaires, and when he received that message from the British Ambassador in Nanking he came to ask my advice as to whether he ought to deliver it to the Japanese Government without instructions from London, because his own Government might regard the step as in the nature of offering mediation, yet the message was too urgent for him to wait for instructions. I told him that he could not possibly take the responsibility of *not* delivering the message immediately, so he did so, and later London approved. The message was delivered to Mr. Horinouchi, who was then Vice Foreign Minister. But it died, alas, and nothing came of it.

History will most certainly take full cognizance of that effort of Chiang Kai-shek for peace. The Japanese forces didn't want an armistice. They have now had war for over four long years with no end in sight. Chiang Kai-shek, a brave and farsighted man, is still the legitimate head of the Chinese Government, is still fighting the ruthless aggression against his country, and Wang Ching-wei could not live a day if Japan's bayonets were withdrawn. How can he therefore be regarded as representative of China or, in fact, anything more than a puppet? I know well Japan's former troubles in China and with China, but those troubles could have been smoothed out eventually by peaceful negotiation. They have not and never will be smoothed out by war which, unless concluded on terms acceptable to the Chinese—also a proud and sensitive people—will make real friendship between Japan and the Chinese impossible for generations to come.

Another and essential aspect of the situation is this. We believe, with abundant reason, that Germany, as controlled by the Nazis, seeks world domination by force and that once in control of Europe and the British Isles it would be only a question of time before the Western Hemisphere was attacked. Hitler has said as much in published statements. We believe that the Nazis seek to control and to alter our whole way of life. Therefore, as a reasonable and sensible measure of self-defense, we determined to help Great Britain to avoid defeat. When Japan allied herself with Germany, we inevitably came to associate Japan with the same general program, so far as the Far East is concerned, and we thereupon determined to assist not only Great Britain but also all other victims of aggression, including China. In pursuing that policy we feel that it would be utterly shortsighted to pour supplies into Great Britain across the Atlantic while complacently watching the potential cutting off of Great Britain's other great life line to the East, which would be accomplished by the fall of Singapore to any Axis power. Therefore, whatever threatens Singapore directly concerns the United States. The occupation of bases in Indo-China definitely does threaten Singapore. The occupation of bases in Thailand would constitute a still more serious threat. Therefore, if Japanese forces should now undertake a further move on the line of the southward advance (and many Japanese openly advocate such a move), I question whether our relations could stand the strain involved.

You mention Iran. The British began to fight this war as amateurs perhaps, but at least like gentlemen. They trusted like gentlemen to Germany's pledged word. But gradually they saw what they were encountering, an enemy whose pledged word meant nothing. In spite of non-aggression pacts and the most solemn assurances given on the very eve of aggression, they saw one country after another fall to the absolutely ruthless invader and to the work of fifth columnists within those countries—Austria, Czechoslovakia, Poland, Belgium, Holland, France, Luxemburg, Denmark, Norway, Rumania, Hungary, Bulgaria, Yugoslavia, Albania, Greece, and now Soviet Russia—as Churchill has so aptly said, "one by one." Do you remember what Hitler said after the seizure of Austria, and after Munich, and after the seizure of Czechoslovakia: "I am now completely satisfied. This is the last territorial readjustment I will seek."! In every case Great Britain was too slow and too late. At last she has wisely learned by bitter experience, and it is that experience which prompted her very wise occupation of Syria and Iran—before Hitler could get there and could threaten the Suez Canal and the whole Mediterranean area. But note the difference: Hitler aims to control all of Europe and has so

xix

stated; Great Britain has pledged herself, and the world by experience can rely on her pledges, to withdraw from Iran and to restore that country's complete sovereignty the moment the necessity for these measures of self-defense has passed. I applaud her action. I cannot admire the action of Japan's allies.

Incidentally, we now learn that the bombing of Iranian cities by either the British or Soviet forces has been officially denied. I am inclined to believe that the bombing report was merely Nazi propaganda.

International relations, if they are to be stable and secure, must be based upon the scrupulous observance of international commitments. Breaking the pledged word between nations can lead only to international anarchy. Was it not the breaking of the Nine-Power Treaty that constituted the first step in this long line of breaches of international commitments by certain nations? It is maintained in Japan that Japan did not break the Nine-Power Treaty. Yet look at the text and the facts, which speak for themselves.

It is held in Japan that under changed conditions that treaty had become obsolete. Very well, our Government has stated in categorical terms that it is ready at all times to consider the effect of changed conditions upon international commitments and to modify or modernize those commitments by peaceful negotiations. We do not regard and never have, as charged, regarded the *status quo* as permanently unalterable. Our negotiations with China for abandoning our extraterritorial rights prove the point, just as does our willingness to surrender our permanent leases in Japan and many other legitimate but outmoded rights. But once Japan resorted to force as an instrument of national policy in breaching an important international treaty—from which Japan had gained much when it was concluded because it was a carefully balanced undertaking, entered

into by Japan freely and, at that time, gladly—a precedent was set and an example was created which were soon followed by other nations, starting, as you will remember, with Italy's action in Ethiopia. This was the beginning of international chaos of which we see the sad result today.

Through the process of publicity and propaganda in Japan, largely stimulated from Axis sources, the Japanese people are today told that the Anglo-Saxon countries propose to "encircle" Japan by their imperialistic ambitions, to obtain complete hegemony in East Asia, to control commerce and trade and sources of raw materials, and to drive Japan to the wall. How untrue is this picture you, my dear friend, know only too well, yet how can we hope to improve our relations so long as the Japanese people are made to believe these preposterous charges? My Government believes, and I believe, that Japan's legitimate interests and aspirations should be given the fullest recognition.

As you know, I am no defeatist. I believe that in spite of present difficulties we can still guide our respective countries into healthy channels, and for that high purpose I am constantly thinking and working. Below are four points which my Government regards as essential for our future good relations. We confidently believe that Japan would achieve the greatest happiness, security, prosperity, and contentment by following a policy of peaceful and productive expansion based on the principle of free and equal treatment for all nations, a policy which would have the full support of the United States, while we believe that the continued use of armed force will lead eventually to social, economic, and financial disaster. These are the points:

1. Respect for the territorial integrity and the sovereignty of each and all nations.

2. Support of the principle of noninterference in the internal affairs of other countries.

3. Support of the principle of equality, including equality of commercial opportunity.

4. Nondisturbance of the *status quo* in the Pacific except as the *status quo* may be altered by peaceful means.

On such a basis and, I fear, only on such a basis will the United States do what you suggest: "ultimately come to sympathize with us in our efforts and, if possible. co-operate with us."

If Japan will mold her policy and actions on the basis of the foregoing four points and will abandon aggression, I see a happy outlook for the development of a new era in Japanese-American relations, contributing to Japan's future prosperity and welfare through a free flow of trade and commerce, access to the needed raw materials, and a successful continuation of industrial development, resulting in a progressive raising of the standard of living of her people and a return to the old cultural values of life which have so brilliantly illuminated her background and history.

We should at all times be aware that the facts of geography are immutable. For better or for worse, Divine Providence has placed our respective nations on either side of the Pacific; we are neighbors for all time to come; and nothing that anyone can do can alter that fact. Since the beginning of relations between our two countries—almost ninety years ago—we have maintained peace between ourselves and, with the exception of the past ten years, our relations have been marked by friendship, good will, and respect, the one for the other. The tradition of good neighborly relations must be restored, for if we fail in that task, there will be introduced into the Pacific the tradition of war which has cursed Europe since the beginning of history. We who are charged with the accomplishment of this task, who are working for the welfare not only of this generation but also of those yet unborn, need your help and the help of all other men of good will.

With expressions of warm friendship, I am as always, my dear ———,

Cordially yours,

JOSEPH C. GREW

President Roosevelt's Message to Congress
Delivered December 8, 1941, Calling for a Declaration of War on Japan

Mr. Vice President, Mr. Speaker, members of the Senate and the House of Representatives:

Yesterday, December 7, 1941—a date which will live in infamy—the United States of America was suddenly and deliberately attacked by naval and air forces of the empire of Japan.

The United States was at peace with that nation, and, at the solicitation of Japan, was still in conversation with its government and its Emperor, looking toward the maintenance of peace in the Pacific.

Indeed, one hour after Japanese air squadrons had commenced bombing in the American island of Oahu the Japanese Ambassador to the United States and his colleague delivered to our Secretary of State a formal reply to a recent American message. And, while this reply stated that it seemed useless to continue the existing diplomatic negotiations, it contained no threat or hint of war or of armed attack.

It will be recorded that the distance of Hawaii from Japan makes it obvious that the attack was deliberately planned many days or even weeks ago. During the intervening time the Japanese Government has deliberately sought to deceive the United States by false statements and expressions of hope for continued peace.

The attack yesterday on the Hawaiian Islands has caused severe dam-

age to American naval and military forces. I regret to tell you that very many American lives have been lost. In addition, American ships have been reported torpedoed on the high seas between San Francisco and Honolulu.

Yesterday the Japanese Government also launched an attack against Malaya.

Last night Japanese forces attacked Hong Kong.

Last night Japanese forces attacked Guam.

Last night Japanese forces attacked the Philippine Islands.

Last night the Japanese attacked Wake Island.

And this morning the Japanese attacked Midway Island.

Japan has therefore undertaken a surprise offensive extending throughout the Pacific area. The facts of yesterday and today speak for themselves. The people of the United States have already formed their opinions and well understand the implications to the very life and safety of our nation.

As Commander in Chief of the Army and Navy I have directed that all measures be taken for our defense, that always will our whole nation remember the character of the onslaught against us.

No matter how long it may take us to overcome this premeditated invasion, the American people, in their righteous might, will win through to absolute victory.

I believe that I interpret the will of the Congress and of the people when I assert that we will not only defend ourselves to the uttermost but will make it very certain that this form of treachery shall never again endanger us.

Hostilities exist. There is no blinking at the fact that our people, our territory, and our interests are in grave danger.

With confidence in our armed forces, with the unbounding determina-

tion of our people, we will gain the inevitable triumph. So help us God.

I ask that the Congress declare that since the unprovoked and dastardly attack by Japan on Sunday, December 7, 1941, a state of war has existed between the United States and the Japanese Empire.

REPORT FROM TOKYO

Return from Japan

LET US put it in a nutshell: there is not sufficient room in the area of the Pacific Ocean for a peaceful America, for any and all of the peace-loving United Nations, and for a swashbuckling Japan.

I shall come back to that subject, but first it may interest you to know something about the last hours in Tokyo preceding the dastardly attack on Pearl Harbor. That story is of important interest.

Late in the evening of December 7, I received a telegram from our Secretary of State, Mr. Hull, containing a message from the President which I was to communicate to the Emperor at the earliest possible moment. I immediately asked for an appointment with the Minister for Foreign Affairs, Mr. Togo, around midnight, and drove at once to the Minister's official residence and requested an audience with the Emperor in order to present the President's message. Mr. Togo said that he would present my request to the Throne, and I left him at about 12:30 A.M. This must have been about two hours—Japan time—prior to the attack on Pearl Harbor.

At 7 A.M. on the morning of December 8, I was awakened by a telephone call from the Foreign Minister's secretary, who asked me to come to the Minister's residence as soon as possible. He said that he had been trying to telephone to me ever since 5 A.M. but had been unable to get connection. I hurriedly dressed and arrived at the official residence at about 7:30. Mr. Togo entered the room grim and formal and handed to me the reply to the President's message to the Emperor, whom I was told he had seen at about 3 A.M., presumably just after the news of the attack on Pearl Harbor. At the same time he handed me a long memorandum ending with the statement: "The Japanese Government regrets to have to notify hereby the American Government that in view of the attitude of the American Government it cannot but consider that it is impossible to reach an agreement through further negotiations." I asked the Minister if he had presented to the Emperor my request for an audience. The Minister merely replied that he had no intention of standing between myself and the Throne. He then made a little speech thanking me for my efforts to preserve peace and as usual came downstairs to see me off at the door. He said nothing whatever about the outbreak of war between our countries, and I returned to the Embassy in entire ignorance that developments more serious than the breaking off of the conversations had occurred. It was not until at least an hour or more later that a press bulletin was released announcing the attack on Hawaii and the outbreak of war between Japan and the United States and Great Britain. When the bulletin was handed to me, I could not believe that the news was true. However, it was soon confirmed from other sources, and later in the morning an official of the Foreign Office brought to my secretary the official note declaring war. Almost immediately afterward the Embassy's gates were closed and locked by the police, and from that moment we were regarded and treated as prisoners. A group of Japanese radio experts then immediately came and went through all our houses with a fine-tooth comb, taking away all short-wave radio sets so that thereafter we should have no contact with the outside world save through the Japanese newspapers, which were regularly delivered to us.

RETURN FROM JAPAN

It was not until almost nine months later that the exchange ship *Gripsholm* brought us up the harbor to New York. Never before has my native land looked to me so beautiful as on that August morning. Never before has a home-coming meant so much. I think you will realize a little of what it meant to us when I tell you of those last seven days at anchor off Yokohama before our evacuation vessel finally sailed from Japanese waters. We were awaiting the completion of the negotiations for our exchange, not knowing whether those negotiations would be successful and whether, if they were unsuccessful, we might not all be returned to our imprisonment in Japan. Among us were many Americans—missionaries, teachers, newspaper correspondents, businessmen—who had spent the preceding six months in solitary confinement in small, bitterly cold prison cells, inadequately clothed and inadequately fed and at times subjected to the most cruel and barbaric tortures. I will not go into the nature of those tortures, which were many, except to mention an incident on the *Gripsholm* when three elderly Americans, one of them over seventy years old, gave me a demonstration of the water cure that had repeatedly been inflicted upon them. We went up the bow of the ship early in the morning, where a friend posed as the subject of the torture. He was tied up with his knees drawn up to his chin, his neck being attached to his knees and his hands securely bound behind him so that the cords in the actual torture had penetrated deep under the skin. He was then rolled over with his face up, and water was poured into his nose and mouth. It was a realistic performance, but only from the oral description of those men could I visualize what the actual torture must have been. Six large buckets of water were used by the Japanese police, so that the subject in every case lost consciousness and then was brought back to consciousness merely to have the same thing repeated. One of those elderly missionaries was given the water cure six separate times in order to make him divulge information which he was supposed to have acquired as an alleged spy. Nearly all of the American missionaries, teachers, newspaper correspondents, and businessmen were regarded as potential spies. The stupidity of those Japanese police was only surpassed by their utter cruelty. That same American told me that once while he was lying tied on the ground, a Japanese had ground his boot sole into his face and then had brutally kicked him, smashing a rib. When he was finally untied, he could barely stand and he said he feared that a rib had been broken. One of the Japanese police asked where the broken rib was and began to feel his body. As the Japanese came to the broken bone he said, "Is that the place?" and when the man answered, "Yes," the policeman hauled off with his fist and hit that broken rib as hard as he could. In another case, a well-known American has been seriously maimed as a result of the gangrene which was caused by the ill-treatment he had received in his prison cell. I had known him in years gone by and seldom have I had so great a shock as when I saw him on the ship, a mere shadow of his former self. There were many, many other cases.

I had heard indirectly of the horrible atrocities perpetrated in the rape of Nanking and of the fearful things done in Hong Kong when soldiers who had been taken as prisoners of war were bayoneted to death. But on shipboard we had direct evidence, for the dying shrieks of those soldiers were heard by a woman, a fellow passenger of ours, who herself told me the terrible story. This was no secondhand evidence, but the reports of reliable firsthand witnesses and, in the case of the torture, the firsthand evidence of those who had suffered the tortures themselves.

Do you wonder that during those seven days of waiting in the harbor of Yokohama several of those people told me that if the negotiations for our exchange failed they would commit suicide rather than return to their imprisonment in Japan? I know that they would have done so.

And then, at the beginning of the eighth day at Yokohama Harbor, came one of the greatest of all moments. I awoke at 1 A.M. on June 25, sensing that something was happening. I looked out of the porthole and saw a piece of wood slowly moving past in the water. Another piece of wood moved faster. We were at last under way, slowly accelerating until the ship was finally speeding at full steam, away from Yokohama, away from Japan, pointing homeward. Ah, what a moment that was, even though we had 18,000 miles to cover and seventy days in all before we should pass the Statue of Liberty in New York Harbor and repeat to ourselves, with tears pouring down many a face:

> *Breathes there the man with soul so dead*
> *Who never to himself hath said,*
> *This is my own, my native land?*

The Japanese military machine against which we are fighting today has been trained and perfected through many years, for it has always had in view, even before the invasion of Manchuria in 1931, the prospect of eventually sweeping not only to the north against Russia, but also far to the west and south. It was their intention to exert Japanese control, politically, economically—absolutely—over all those far-flung territories.

In 1931 came their invasion of Manchuria. In 1937 came their invasion of China south of the wall, and while their Army eventually floundered in China, due to the magnificent fighting spirit of Chiang Kai-shek, his courageous armies, and his determined people, nevertheless the warfare which then ensued proved a practical training for the Japanese soldiers

7

and sailors, who tirelessly developed and perfected the tactics they subsequently used in their landings and conquests to the south.

The idea should not for a moment be entertained that the failure of the Japanese forces in China has discouraged the Japanese people. It has instead served to steel them for still-greater sacrifices and to prepare them better for the war of deadly purpose to conquer upon which they have finally embarked. As the realization came home to them of the need for greater and greater efforts, they accepted the inevitable war-footing reorganization of the country's life with characteristic calmness and determination.

Probably no other factor has contributed more heavily to the preliminary victories achieved by the Japanese in this war than the offensive spirit which permeates all of the armed forces of the Empire. This spirit, recognized by competent military men as the most vital intangible factor in achieving victory, has been nourished and perpetuated since the foundation of the modern Japanese Army. The Japanese High Command has counted heavily upon the advantages this would give them over less aggressive enemies. They attach great importance to the former disunity in the United States over the war issue and they still count on an appreciable interval before an aroused nation can find itself and develop a fighting spirit of its own. By that time, they feel, Japan will be in complete control of all East Asia. When they struck, they made no provision for failure; they left no road open for retreat. They struck with all the force and power at their command. And they will continue to fight in the same manner until they are utterly crushed.

We shall crush that machine and caste and system in due course, but if we Americans think that, collectively and individually, we can continue to lead our normal lives, leaving the spirit of self-sacrifice to our soldiers and sailors, letting the intensification of our production program take care of itself, we shall unquestionably risk the danger of a stalemate in this war of ours with Japan. I say this in the light of my ten years' experience in Japan, my knowledge of the power of the Japanese Army and Navy and of the hardness and fighting spirit of the Japanese. I feel it my bounden duty to say this to my fellow countrymen. I know my own country even better than I know Japan and I have not the slightest shadow of doubt of our eventual victory. But I do not wish to see the period of our blood, sweat, and tears *indefinitely and unnecessarily prolonged*. That period will be prolonged only if our people fail to realize the truth of what I have just said, that we are up against a powerful fighting machine, a people whose morale cannot and will not be broken even by successive defeats, who will certainly not be broken by economic hardships, a people who individually and collectively will gladly sacrifice their lives for their Emperor and their nation, and who can be brought to earth only by physical defeat, by being ejected physically from the areas which they have temporarily conquered or by a progressive attrition of their naval power and merchant marine which will finally result in cutting off their homeland from all connection with and access to those outlying areas—by complete defeat in battle.

The truth as I see it from long experience and observation is this: nothing less than the exertion of our maximum capacities, individually and collectively, in a war of offense will bring our beloved country safely through these deep waters to the longed-for haven of a victorious peace.

I have lived for ten years in Japan. I have had many friends in Japan, some of whom I admired, respected, and loved. They are not the people who brought on this war. As patriots they will fight for their Emperor and country, to the last ditch if necessary, but they did not want this war and it was not they who began it. Even during the imprisonment in Tokyo of the American Embassy staff after Pearl Harbor, many of those friends used to contrive to send us gifts, in spite of the usual obstruction of the police, who wished to cut us off completely from the outside world. They were not the usual gifts of flowers but gifts of food, sometimes a piece of meat, which was the most precious gift they could confer because they themselves could seldom get meat. For ten years I have broken bread in their houses and they in mine. They were personally loyal to me to the end.

But there is the other side to the picture, the ugly side of cruelty, brutality, and utter bestiality, the ruthlessness and rapaciousness of the Japanese military machine which brought on this war. That Japanese military machine and military caste and military system must be utterly crushed, their credit and predominance must be utterly broken, for the future safety and welfare of the United States and of the United Nations, and for the future safety and welfare of civilization and humanity. Surely ours is a cause worth sacrificing for and living for and dying for, if necessary.

> *Though love repine and reason chafe,*
> *There came a voice without reply:*
> *" 'Tis man's perdition to be safe,*
> *When for the truth he ought to die."*

2

Why War Came

JAPAN FACES ruin. The problem that confronts us is, on the one hand, how do we escape being drawn down into it? It would be small comfort to us to see Japan eaten up by a monstrous militarism if the same militarism devoured us. Canada and the United States cannot stand apart from the destiny of the peoples on the other side of the Pacific. Either Japan destroys us all, including the Japanese people themselves, or we destroy the militarism of Japan and win for all the Pacific peoples the just and free society which we believe to be the rightful condition of all nations.

When I say that Japan is ruined I offer no glib assurance of our triumph in the cause of democracy and human progress. I mean only that, even if Japan were to win the war—which it surely will not—the Japanese people would face the ruin of their business and their social system.

If they were to win, they would be still as they are today, enslaved by their own leaders. The faltering steps they have made toward constitutionalism, toward humanitarianism, would be undone. Pawns under a senseless but mighty militarism, they would turn toward a new age of darkness blacker than any that they had known before.

On the other hand, when Japan loses, they will pay the price of false war. Over and above the obligations they have incurred to the invaded nations, they will owe themselves a debt—a debt of economic spoliation for this vain war, of Japanese already dead and the millions more who must and will die, of the confusion that will beset them when they realize the falsehood and tragedy of the slogan that their leaders have "sold" them, the "Greater East Asia Co-Prosperity Sphere." Surely we have had ample evidence—in Korea, in Formosa, in Manchuria, and in other parts of occupied China—of Japan's interpretation of the euphemistic term "Co-Prosperity." I need not elaborate that subject.

There are many questions which we have been asking ourselves since the grim forenoon of December 7, 1941. Some of these questions will be answered only by the historians of the far future. Why did Japan attack the United States and the British Commonwealth of Nations? Why did the Japanese wish to destroy us? Why did they risk the venture of war with our peoples, who are known for industrial power and for potential military capacity? Did the Japanese indeed make the most monumental miscalculation in all history? Are they foolish fanatics who have chosen a suicidal war as the only way out from their humiliation by Chinese resistance? Questions such as these have been asked me ever since my return from Tokyo.

I fear, alas, that no man living could answer all of these questions. If there is anyone who knows all the answers, I for one would like to learn from him. I know that there are many important points about the Japanese mind and spirit which have puzzled and troubled me, and which are probably not clear to the Japanese themselves. Nevertheless, I will put before you two of the main questions, and try to give answers to them which I believe come near to the heart of the matter.

First, why did the Japanese make this war upon us?

Second, how do the Japanese leaders—fanatical but coldly calculating

men—dare dream of victory over the combined power of the British Commonwealth of Nations, the United States, China, and the other United
Nations?

Why did they make war upon us? The Japanese attitude toward the
English-speaking peoples is based on a concept of Japanese superiority
and strength and of our inferiority and weakness. Part of this is a product
of their mythology—the only neolithic mythology in the world which still
plays a part in the affairs of a government. A part of it is a product of
national vanity. A part of it is—in the Japanese view—logical, matter-of-
fact, and well founded.

It is a paradox of Japanese thinking that, despite their faith in their
own innate superiority, they believe that the man who thinks he is superior is *ipso facto* handicapped. The Japanese have known what we thought
of them—that they were little fellows physically, that they were imitative,
that they were not really very important in the world of men and nations.
Believe me, I have been shamed more than once by the braggadocio, self-
confidence, and condescension manifested by our English-speaking peoples; and I have grown apprehensive as, through the years, I have
observed the Japanese observing us. I have realized the cold, withering
contempt of the Japanese for those of our race who gloried in power without possessing the fundamentals of power, or who complacently viewed
the possibility of war with Japan without understanding how formidable
the Japanese really were.

The Japanese have made comparisons not favorable to us. They have
pointed to their own thrift and compared it with our wastefulness. They
have looked at their own national unity and national reverence and have
contrasted it with our partisanship and our readiness to laugh at ourselves. They have seen the comforts with which we have surrounded

ourselves, and they envy us these even while they despise us for our possession and enjoyment of them.

It is not meaningless that in Japanese thought "Oriental culture" stands as the antithesis to luxury. To many Japanese, culture means a Spartan ability to endure hard work, hard living, and hard fighting. The inconsistency of their position—the fact that they should pride themselves on their simplicity and ruggedness while fighting to gain material riches —is not apparent to most of them. They look upon us as boastful, vainglorious, rich, and flabby. They think that we are physically soft. They think that our minds are filled with gross considerations of comfort, personal greed, and shallow partisanship.

I have no wish to praise a people who are our enemies, but I must—in the interests of our safety—list a few of their formidable characteristics:

They are united. Theirs is a unity of solidarity. Foolish or wise though their war government may be, they support it. They believe in the divinity of their Emperor and, through him, in the rightness of their war leaders. For years they have prepared themselves collectively and individually for war. Germany and Italy possess groups of unknown size and power which await only the time and opportunity to revolt. In Japan there are no such groups.

They are trained. The Japanese have said openly that their weapons were inferior to ours but they counted on the fact that we supposed them to be even less well equipped than they really were. This would give them an advantage. This advantage could be further supplemented by their discipline, by their universal training, and by the fact that all Japanese men—all the able-bodied men in Japan—have military service. Trained men and armies with fair weapons can often defeat untrained men and armies with excellent weapons.

They are frugal. The Japanese Empire has almost thrived on shortages. Bottlenecks, absences of materials, and vexing priorities have existed in other countries under conditions which would have meant abundance to the Japanese. In the midst of poverty, they have built an enormous military machine. They have not done this with wastefulness. They have done it with care and thrift and economy and conserving of materials. The food which we, even now, throw away in North America would go a long way toward supporting the population of Japan.

They are fanatical. They believe in their war, in the government which wages it, and in the incorruptible certainty of their national cause. Who knows how far back the sources of this national faith may lie? Some parts of it go back to the half-mythical centuries of their history before the time of Christ. Others rest, perhaps, in the centuries of sporadic struggles with the Chinese which ended with the great naval victories of the seventh-century Chinese fleets. The shoguns, who began the system of ruling through puppets a thousand years ago, and then the feudal lords, contributed their share. Medieval civil wars, then, bequeathed traditions which toughened Japan for foreign war today.

They are, at least in war, totalitarian. Long ago, while Germany and Italy were still picturesque agglomerations of petty states, Japan was governed by dictatorship, secret police, elite guards, suppressors of "dangerous thoughts," summary courts, and hidden executioners. The Tokugawa shogunate, which preceded the present modernized government, was effectively totalitarian and authoritarian.

We have learned in our time what totalitarianism means. It means the end of political freedom, of religious freedom, of any freedom, of any true culture. It also means concentrated political, economic, and military power. This power can be used swiftly and ruthlessly by despots who do not stop to explain—still less to justify—their ends or their means. Japan did not have to turn Fascist or National Socialist; morally, Japan already was both. Japan has needed no Hitler. In a certain sense, her militarists are an oligarchy of Hitlers. Democracy was an experiment into which the Japanese ventured only slightly and cautiously. The society itself, and its values, remain today, in wartime, regimented and authoritarian.

With such capacities, and such a government, is it surprising that Japan's leaders did not fear war and that they led their nation confidently into war? At this very moment, the Japanese feel themselves, man for man, superior to you and to me and to any of our peoples. They admire our technology, they may have a lurking dread of our ultimate superiority of resources, but all too many of them have contempt for us as human beings. Add to all this their overweening ambition for conquest, and you can begin to follow the warped but persuasive lines of intuition and belief which led Japan to attack us.

Yet we now try to give an answer to the second question: do the Japanese think that they can win this war?

The Japanese leaders *do* think that they can and will win. They are counting on our underestimates, on our apparent disunity before—and even during—war, on our unwillingness to sacrifice, to endure, and to fight.

The leaders of Japan are not suicidally minded incompetents. History will show that they have made a miscalculation; but they have miscalculated less than most of us suppose. In this they find strength.

Japan has won before by the same strategy that she has followed in launching and waging this war. In 1894 and 1895, Japan defeated the gigantic Manchu Empire of China. Her armed forces won because the

16

nation was prepared, united, determined. The Manchu court of China was corrupt and unprepared, the Chinese Government was supine and disunited, and the Chinese people never had a chance to fight. In 1904 and 1905, Japan attacked and defeated the Empire of the Tsars. Her armed forces attacked Port Arthur, like Pearl Harbor, murderously and in stealth. Port Arthur, like Bataan, withstood a siege and then surrendered. In St. Petersburg and Moscow there was revolt, occasioned largely by the corrupt mismanagement of the war and a popular distrust of the government. The Tsarist Government negotiated peace. Japan could not have defeated *Russia;* she did defeat the Tsarist forces when the people and government behind the armed forces were disunited and the productive system did not stand up. Later, I saw disunion and defeat lingering on in St. Petersburg; and the unhappy remembrance of it has remained in my mind to this day. Finally, Japan, as one of the Allies, fought Germany in the First World War. Germany did not fight to the bitter end. The Germans did not wait for their country to be invaded. They gave in before the Rhine had even been reached—they surrendered even after they had won the Eastern front and had seemed victorious. The Japanese noted this and did not forget it.

Japan remembers these victories. As I have already stated, the Japanese may not intend to take New Orleans or San Francisco or Vancouver or Toronto—in this war. They do intend and expect, in dead seriousness, to conquer Asia, to drive us out, to force us to make a peace which will weaken us, and cause us to grow weaker with time. And then later, in five years, or ten years, or fifty years, they would use the billion men of an enslaved Asia, and all the resources of the East, to strike again.

There is no limit to the Japanese desire for conquest. Given this desire, given their estimate of us, the attack on Pearl Harbor was a logical development. Our Government was aware of this. The closure of commercial relations and the scale of our rearmament—late though this was—were influenced by that knowledge.

When the Japanese militarists, committed absolutely to the course of conquest, took measure of their military resources and perceived the extent of democratic rearmament, they had to gamble. The gamble was heroic, but not that of a mere game of chance. Their well-planned campaigns southward were brilliant accomplishments. Today Japan is stronger than ever. We now face not only Japan, but Japan and Japan's conquests. These conquests are greater than we have permitted ourselves to realize. They include more than ten times the area of the Japanese Empire as it stood a year ago—Chinese territory, British territory, Dutch territory, American territory. They include populations aggregating three times the population of the Japanese Empire. Many climes and vast resources. A huge aggregate of human beings, the majority of whom are docile and are capable of tremendous toil. True, we are counterattacking. Canadian and American planes are hammering at the Japanese in the Aleutians. British and American planes are striking at the Japanese in Burma. Chinese and American planes are bombing points in occupied China. Australian and American planes are counterattacking in the South Pacific. But Japan is on the inner circle and she is busily developing the resources and the man power that she has seized.

No one—any longer—can prattle now of defeating Japan in three months. We hear no longer about the tinder cities of Tokyo and Osaka. We do not jest about the Japanese fleet, or about their Air Force. We know that we face a destructive, united enemy, and that we must bring to bear against that enemy force as united as and greater than that which he has marshaled.

3

The Extent of the Japanese Challenge

FROM MANY talks with many different elements of our people since my return, I have sensed the most earnest desire of all to contribute, individually and collectively, their maximum potentialities of service to our national effort toward winning this war. But many of those with whom I have talked seem to have no real comprehension of what we are up against, no real comprehension that we are not fighting distant enemies merely to preserve our national "interests" but, in fact, to preserve our national life—our existence as a free and sovereign people. There are certain salient facts concerning the widely misunderstood effectiveness and power and the all-out, do-or-die fanatical spirit of the Japanese military machine against which we are fighting today. Unless that effectiveness and power and spirit are correctly assessed by the American people as a whole, our road to victory will be doubly long and hard and bloody.

Many have said to me that the American people are ready but that our leaders must show us the way. Show the way? If anyone feels that our leaders have not pointed out the way, let him read again and again the statements and declarations of our President, of our Vice-President, of our Secretary of State, and of our other high officials, with the fullest support and co-operation of many other leaders of public thought. Haven't our leaders month in and month out given us our bearings, charted our course, told us what lay ahead, what we now are fighting for and what we may expect if we fail in that fight? Haven't they asked for our maximum efforts in production, for our individual and collective self-sacrifice of the nonessentials of life, for hard thinking and resolute action on our part, not in terms of our daily convenience but of our daily contribution? Why waste invaluable time and energy in bickering about details, about non-essentials? Why not let come to the fore and give full play to our American initiative and resourcefulness and the inherent toughness of earlier diffi-cult days? A very great number of our fellow countrymen are imbued with the finest spirit of self-sacrifice and determination to go all out in their war effort. They are wide awake and functioning to their full ca-pacities. Others among our fellow countrymen are similarly eager to serve but are not yet fully awake to the realities of the situation. They have failed to analyze the dangers which confront us or to realize the full grimness and potential desperate demands of this war which we are wag-ing actually to preserve our liberty—waging to preserve the very prin-ciple of liberty. Others among our fellow countrymen are quite simply still asleep.

Since coming back to Washington I have seen at close hand, personally and intimately, the grim determination and decisiveness of those leaders of ours. The problems they have to face are among the greatest and most difficult in the history of our nation. But those problems, one by one, are being faced and dealt with in that very spirit of determination and de-cisiveness which fills me with patriotic pride. I was in Washington in 1917. The war effort of our country then was amateurish compared with our war effort now. I have talked directly with the officers of our joint Chiefs of Staff, with large groups of our Army and Navy officers, with the production management, with the members of our strategic services, and with many others from the President down. Some of their problems seem almost insuperable, but the spirit of their determination to solve those problems is absolutely invincible, and they *are* solving them, hour by hour and day by day. If only our people, our people as a whole, will realize the dangers which we are up against, what we stand to lose by failure, what we must and will gain by victory—if only our people as a whole will get in and push to the maximum of their several capacities!

Let us look at one aspect of Japanese life. There is nothing unusual to us about free workers and free management assembling in a free country. Benjamin Franklin once said that we never miss the water until the well runs dry. I have spent the last ten years in a country where the well of liberty has always been dry. Nowhere in Japan is the worker more than an unresisting pawn of the militarists who are driving his country to destruction.

The Japanese worker has nothing to say about his wages, which before the war were barely enough for his subsistence, and still undoubtedly are. He has nothing to say about his hours, which are long and backbreaking. If he has any union at all, it dare not lift its voice. It has been driven underground by the brutal methods of the "thought control" police. In fact, there is almost nothing that he has any say about, from the moment that he comes into the world until the moment when, worn out by unhealthful working conditions, long hours, and poor diet, he takes his leave of it forever.

This is what it means to be a worker in Japan. This, or far worse, is what it means to be a worker in any country which falls before Japan's armed forces.

Yet we must not be misled by the abject poverty and regimentation of our enemies. The conditions I have described would lead free Americans to revolt. But Japan is a country far different from our own in every conceivable way. Under these conditions the Japanese workers have docilely toiled to build a military machine which has swept across eastern Asia like a tidal wave and will sweep still farther if allowed to do so.

The Japanese people have been accustomed to regimentation since the very birth of their nation. There are Japanese living today who were born when their country was still a feudal land, when every feudal lord held the power of life and death over his so-called common people. We in the West shook off feudalism many centuries ago. In Japan it existed so recently that it has left a vast heritage of almost prostrate subservience to birth and authority.

The men who rule Japan today have taken full advantage of the docility of the Japanese people to create a formidable military and economic machine. If a man will yield himself to hypnotism, it is as easy to convince him that he is a roaring tiger as to make him believe he is a gentle lamb. The Japanese militarists have hypnotized their fellow countrymen into believing they are roaring tigers, and they will continue to try to act like tigers until the black spell has been broken.

These ruthless architects of aggression have carried out their plans with diabolical cleverness. Their campaign of propaganda has been long and incessant. Even Japan's handicaps have been used to strengthen her for war. The low standard of living of the Japanese people, for example, has been used to inure them to a Spartan life. Today the Japanese soldier on the fighting front, the Japanese sailor in his cramped ship, and the Japanese worker in his gloomy factory can alike live on a diet so meager that any American on the same diet would soon collapse. The traditional subservience to authority has been used to lead the Japanese workers to accept a degree of regimentation that in some respects exceeds that of better-

22

known Nazi Germany. And this regimented industrial machine has been turned to one purpose—the production of the tools of war. The very failure of Japan's war against China has been used to induce the Japanese people to accept placidly severe measures of control and rationing—measures of such severity that without the psychology of war they would surely lead to revolt.

Above all, the men who rule Japan have used their efficient propaganda machine to instill in every Japanese a fanatical devotion to his country. Even those who hate their nation's entry into this present war have buried their personal feelings. Even they have come to accept the belief that the future of their country depends upon the outcome of the war. We would be deluding ourselves if we believed that any personal sacrifices which the Japanese people might be called upon to make would lead to any cracking of their morale. Yamato Damashi—the spirit of Japan—has been stronger during recent months than ever before. The undeniable successes of their armies, sweeping across Malaya, Burma, the Philippines, the Netherlands East Indies, and many of the islands of the southwest Pacific, have given them tremendous confidence in their ability to win. They know that they have a long and difficult fight before them. They believe that by grim endurance they will grasp victory.

This confidence is based not only on the successes of their own forces, but also on false contempt for the fighting ability of their enemies. The Japanese are well aware of the technical achievements of the Western powers—so well aware, indeed, that they have taken many of these achievements and adapted them to their own use. They are well aware of the high standard of living of Western peoples. But they believe that this high standard has brought a softness—even a degeneracy—to Western civilization. This is the real challenge to America—the challenge of a people who have been hypnotized into believing that democracy weakens those who possess it, that a high standard of living weakens those who enjoy it, that peace and the love of peace weaken those who cherish them. Too long have we nurtured the illusion that the Japanese is an insignificant person whose achievements are poor imitations of our own achievements. He is a clever and dangerous enemy—one who will compel us to use all the intelligence and all the strength of which we are capable in order to bring about his defeat.

And as for us, what is our answer to this challenge from across the Pacific? What is our reply to these little islanders who believe that we are weak and of divided mind in our hour of peril?

I do not know that I have been back in the United States long enough to have a final answer to this question. But I do believe that I have seen enough and talked to enough people to get something of the feel of my native country in this year of crisis. Perhaps the very fact that I have been away from America for some time may enable me to see somewhat more clearly the changes that have taken place in the transition from peace to war than if I had been here to live through them from day to day.

No one returning to this country after a long absence can fail to be impressed by the way our great industrial capacity has been converted to the production of munitions. No one can fail to be impressed by the vast armies which are being mustered around us and the great fleets which are being hammered into shape. But we have by no means neared the limits of achievement. What we have done to date, we have accomplished through the comparatively easy, first stages of transformation of our industrial machinery and our vast store of man power from the purposes of peace to those of war. We are like a football team running through its practice plays against the scrubs. The players carry out their assignments;

but the punch, the determined plunge that brings victory in the big game, is lacking. We must pull ourselves up short. Let us make no mistake. This is the real thing, played for keeps. An easygoing transformation is not enough. Our effort must be an extraordinary one—one which exceeds anything that we have undertaken heretofore. In winning this broad continent which is our heritage, in preserving it from attack within and without, the American people in the past have performed the tasks of giants. Today we face the greatest task in our history.

A friend of mine recently wrote me: "You will find this country sound in feeling, but still unable to realize that we are involved in a desperate war."

I need not recount for you how our men on the firing lines face to face with the enemy, and our women behind those lines—with their spirit, determination, effectiveness, and sacrifice—are beating back the enemy's ambitious will to conquer. They at the fighting fronts can handle anything the Japanese can send against them if, and it is an important "if," each and every one of us—you and I—gives them his utmost support. The ruthless will which is driving the Japanese nation toward conquest knows neither gentleness nor mercy. It is utterly ruthless, utterly cruel, and utterly blind to any of the values which make up our civilization. The only way to stop that will is to destroy it.

If we fail—please mark my words—we pass into slavery, and all the world passes into slavery with us. But we will not fail; we will not fail—because we are free men living in a free country, able and determined that we, our country, shall remain free, that our homes, our traditions, our civilization, our principles, our standards, our humanity, shall remain free—and that henceforth we shall also be and shall remain secure.

4

How We Must Fight to Defeat Japan

IN NOVEMBER, 1939, at a time when the Japanese Army was floundering unsuccessfully in China, I wrote in my diary: "To await the hoped-for discrediting in Japan of the Japanese Army and the Japanese military system is to await the millennium. The Japanese Army is no protuberance like the tail of a dog that might be cut off to prevent the tail from wagging the dog. It is inextricably bound up with the fabric of the entire nation. Certainly there are plenty of Japanese who dislike the Army's methods; there is plenty of restiveness at the wholesale impressment of young men to fight in China, at the death and crippling of many, and at the restrictions and handicaps in everyday life entailed by the expenses of the China campaign. But that the Army can be discredited in the eyes of the people to a degree where its power and prestige will become so effectively undermined as to deprive it of control, or at least of its preponderant influence in shaping national policy, is an hypothesis which I believe no one conversant with Japan and the Japanese would for a moment entertain.

"Should a *coup d'état* occur in Japan through social upheaval, there is little doubt that it would lead immediately to a ruthless military dictatorship."

That entry in my diary was made three years ago. A good deal of water has run under the mill since then, but those comments are just as true today as they were then—except in one fundamental respect. I then wrote that the Japanese Army was inextricably bound up with the life of the people, and when I wrote of the Army I alluded to the whole great military machine, which includes the Navy too. So it is today. From every village and farm and factory and home, sons and brothers and fellow workers have been taken for military or naval service throughout the nation. That whole machine is closely integrated with every phase of the national life. But I also wrote at that time that that military machine could not be discredited in the eyes of the people. Today I amend that statement. The Japanese military machine can and will be discredited in the eyes of the Japanese people—and we, the United States of America, will bring that about.

Two questions. First, why? Answer: because until it is so discredited, permanent peace never can and never will be restored in the Pacific area. Second, how? Answer: by utter and complete defeat by the armed forces of the United States of America and of the other United Nations. Only when that Japanese military machine is rendered physically impotent, physically incapable of carrying on its far-flung campaign of crushing and conquering and enslaving those who fall beneath the wheels of its ruthless and utterly pitiless car of Juggernaut, only then will the Japanese people as a whole come to the realization that crime does not pay, that they have been forced to follow false gods, and that the ways of peace are in all respects preferable to the ways of war. And when that time comes, as it assuredly will come in due course, many a Japanese, many a patriotic and loyal Japanese, loyal to his Emperor, loyal to the spirits of his ancestors, and loyal to his nation, yet who did not want this war, who had nothing whatever to do with the bringing on of this war, will sigh with profoundest relief.

27

Now how is that defeat to be brought about? Our strategists and tacticians will take care of that. As a layman in military and naval matters, I should say that two main courses will have to be followed simultaneously. First, the gradual but progressive dislodgment of the Japanese forces from the bases and areas that they have temporarily occupied. You know from the published reports what our marines, our sailors, our soldiers, our ships, and our planes are doing in the South Seas today. They have a tough job ahead, but they themselves are made of iron. *They* will not fail. Second, the gradual but progressive destruction of the Japanese Navy, merchant marine, and Air Force—producing an attrition which must finally so reduce and weaken their combatant power and their attenuated lines of supply that the homeland will be isolated from every area which they have occupied. This will not be the end, but it will be the beginning of the end. Let us leave the *coup de grâce* to our tacticians. *They* will not fail.

And how about the rest of us? Shall *we* fail? Shall we fail so to integrate our war effort into the life of the nation that our men and boys, valiantly fighting overseas against that all-powerful and equally valiant enemy, shall be deprived of a single ship or plane or gun or shell that *might* have reached them but did not reach them because in some respects our efforts at home had been geared to our creditable but not our *maximum* capacity?

The other day a friend, an intelligent American, said to me: "Of course there must be ups and downs in this war; we can't expect victories every day; but it's merely a question of time before Hitler will go down to defeat before the steadily growing power of the combined air and naval and military forces of the United Nations—and then, we'll mop up the Japs." Mark well those words, please. "And then we'll mop up the Japs."

HOW WE MUST FIGHT TO DEFEAT JAPAN

Let's get down to brass tacks. I know Germany; I lived there for nearly ten years. I came out on the last train with my chief, Ambassador Gerard, when in 1917 we broke relations with Germany and shortly afterward were forced to declare war on that aggressor. I know the Germans well; truculent and bullying and domineering when on the crest of the wave; demoralized in defeat. The Germans cracked in 1918. I have steadfastly believed and I believe today that when the tide of battle turns against them as it assuredly will turn, they will crack again.

I know Japan; I lived there for ten years. I know the Japanese intimately. The Japanese will not crack. They will not crack morally or psychologically or economically, even when eventual defeat stares them in the face. They will pull in their belts another notch, reduce their rations from a bowl to a half bowl of rice, and fight to the bitter end. Only by utter physical destruction or utter exhaustion of their men and materials can they be defeated. That is the difference between the Germans and the Japanese. That is what we are up against in fighting Japan.

We must realize that the Japanese are already in the Aleutian Islands. Not far from Alaska. Not so far from other parts of our country. Our own armed forces are dealing with that situation. I mention it merely as a concrete indication of what the armed forces of Japan hope to do, and what they intend to do—and what they will do if they can. First to bomb important American centers and then, eventually, invade America.

There is a little story that throws light upon the spirit which animates these grim warriors. Last year when our country and Japan were still at peace, I received from the Chinese Government the name of a Japanese who had been taken prisoner in China and who wished his family at home in Japan to know that he was alive and well. I communicated the information to the Government in Tokyo and received, in due course, the official reply. It was brief and to the point. The Japanese Government was not interested in receiving such information. So far as they, the Government, were concerned, and also so far as his own family was concerned, that man was officially dead. Were he to be recognized as a prisoner of war, shame would be brought upon not only his own family, but also his Government and his nation. "Victory or death" is no mere slogan for these soldiers. It is a plain, matter-of-fact description of the military policy that controls their forces, from the highest generals to the newest recruit. The man who allows himself to be captured has disgraced himself and his country.

Let us take a somewhat more intimate and extensive look at this Army which today is hoping to bivouac on the White House lawn.* The Japanese Army has one great advantage over her enemies in the Far East—the advantage of five years of hard fighting in the China war. They have paid dearly for it. Estimates of their casualties run as high as a million men. But for this grim price in blood they obtained a proving ground where they could build a tough, veteran army trained in that greatest of all military schools—war itself.

But the Japanese were not content with this. They gave their men further training in special areas where the terrain and climatic conditions approximate those in the regions where they were to fight. The units and commanders for the various sectors were selected months in advance and put to work. The Malayan army trained in Hainan and Indo-China, the Philippine force in Formosa, and both units practiced landing operations during the late summer and fall of 1941 along the South China coast. Even the divisions chosen to attack Hong Kong were given rigorous training in night fighting and in storming pill boxes in the hills near

* The material immediately following is based on an admirable report by Lieutenant Colonel C. Stanton Babcock, Assistant Military Attaché in Tokyo.

Canton. So realistic were these maneuvers that the troops are reported to have suffered "a number of casualties."

The Japanese High Command was able to make these careful preparations because of years of study of the areas where they expected to wage future campaigns. This study was based on a first-class espionage system. Japanese commentators have not even attempted to hide the fact that the High Command was fully informed for a year before the war of the strength, dispositions, and likely plans of their potential enemies. A good deal of this information is said to have been obtained by "observing" maneuvers in the Philippines and in Malaya. We can seriously question whether much of this information was gathered by official observers. The eyes of the High Command were probably reserve officers, disguised as humble members of the Japanese community scattered throughout the world.

In making use of this highly valuable information, the various branches of the Japanese armed forces—land, sea, and air—worked together in complete unity. This was the more surprising, inasmuch as the great political activity of both armed services in Tokyo had led to a considerable amount of suspicion and jealousy on the home front. Apparently none of it carried over to the fighting front, for Japanese Army-Navy teamwork left nothing to be desired. "Task forces" organized during the summer of 1941 trained and worked together continuously. Details of command, supply, and other matters which might have given rise to controversy were carefully worked out in advance and clearly understood by all concerned.

In developing these task forces, great importance was laid upon the attainment of air superiority. Admitting frankly their enemies' greater potential air power, the Japanese nevertheless believed that they could seize, and maintain for a long time, command of the air in East Asia. Once again, events proved them right. Air Force units, both of the Army and of the Navy, concentrated their strength against enemy airfields, and not until the opposing air strength was thoroughly crushed was any considerable part of the available Japanese forces diverted to other missions.

The use of dive and light bombers as a kind of long-range artillery was closely patterned on German tactics, as the Japanese themselves admit. This flying artillery was especially effective in the early stages of the Malayan campaign, where the terrain made observation difficult and the emplacement of large numbers of ground batteries was virtually impossible.

The Japanese have borrowed more from the Germans than their tactics in the use of dive and light bombers. Like the Nazi High Command, they refuse to admit that there are any natural obstacles that their forces cannot cross. How often have the German armies shown how the Allied commanders had made the mistaken assumption that terrain that is merely difficult is impassable! In their lightning campaigns of last winter, the Japanese made the same point over and over again. Indeed, the Japanese themselves have said that their tactics have frequently been based on the principle of attacking through a particular area in the knowledge that their enemies have been lulled into a false sense of security and complacency by the very assumption of its impassability. And the Japanese emphasize the disastrous effect on the defenders' morale once a so-called impregnable area has been pierced.

But above all, according to both the Japanese themselves and outside observers, the most important factor contributing to Japanese victories is the spirit which permeates all the armed forces of the Empire. This spirit, recognized by competent military men as the most vital intangible factor in achieving victory, has been nourished and perpetuated since the foundation of the modern Japanese Army. But the Japanese have been careful to develop a tremendous fighting spirit in their armed services and people alike. Indeed, the Japanese armed services and the Japanese nation have become so closely identified that it is difficult to tell where one stops and the other begins. Every Japanese male, of course, must perform military service under a system of universal conscription. Thus in every family, the father or son or brother has served or is serving in the Army or Navy. Every house in Japan, down to the lowliest hovel, proudly flies the Japanese flag at its front door when one of its men is in military service.

The people of Japan are wholly united in their support of their armed forces and of this war simply because it is declared to be the will of the Emperor. To oppose the will of the Throne, the will of the Son of Heaven, is unthinkable in Japan. Disloyalty to the Emperor, too, would shame their own ancestors; and ancestor worship, the patriotic faith called Shintoism, is the fundamental faith of the entire country.

Not that the Japanese Government has ever succeeded in obtaining universal conformity among its subjects. Even among the Japanese there are a few bold spirits who are unwilling to accept dictation from above and who insist on thinking for themselves. There could be no attitude more dangerous to an autocracy, and all such thoughts are labeled by the Japanese police as "dangerous thoughts." Many a Japanese finds himself in a solitary prison cell, undergoing long months of intensive investigation, on the basis of a mere indiscreet word uttered in the hearing of some stranger or even friend.

We may well ask ourselves how so many of our people came to pay so little attention to this formidable military machine—a machine which dominated the lives of the Japanese people long before Pearl Harbor. Partly, of course, we can lay it to our remoteness as a nation from the place where this machine was in action. This remoteness served not only to keep us from obtaining firsthand impressions of the activities of the Japanese Army, but also to lull us into a false sense of security. Many believed that because the Pacific was between us and Japan we were safe. That thought was relentlessly hammered home here in America by the head-in-the-sand school of political leaders. I may add that it was with considerable joy that the leaders of Japan observed what I am sure was the unintentional co-operation of the American isolationists in Japan's plans to fool us. Often have I seen the public speeches of those isolationists flaunted under big headlines in the Japanese press.

Nevertheless, the Japanese ability in deception and concealment played a very considerable part in keeping our people ignorant of the true meaning of what was going on in eastern Asia. Many, for example, took the apparent failure of the Japanese Army to drive to victory in the four years of the China war as evidence of the weakness and inefficiency of the Japanese military forces. It has become more and more apparent since Pearl Harbor that, however much we hoped for peace in Asia, the Japanese themselves throughout the China war were husbanding their resources for the greater struggle which they felt lay beyond. In this connection, the Japanese budget figures released to the press are extremely interesting. They indicate that only forty per cent of the appropriation voted to the defense forces was expended for the conduct of the so-called China "incident." Sixty per cent—nearly two thirds of the total appropriation—was used to prepare the services and the industrial plants for the greater emergency yet to come. Similarly, of the materials and weapons furnished the services, only one fifth was sent to China—the rest being used to expand and modernize the armies and fleets which were to be called upon when the superwar really broke.

Oversimplified and inconclusive though these figures are, the Japanese themselves nevertheless use them to support their promise that the war in China has left Japan stronger rather than weaker and in a better position than ever before to strike at her enemies.

Nevertheless, despite its strength, Japan's new empire should certainly not be considered invulnerable. It has definite weaknesses which, if we take full advantage of them, will lead ultimately to the collapse of her whole position.

Japan, despite an unparalleled expansion over an area of many thousands of square miles in the campaigns of the past winter, has not succeeded in removing strong Allied positions on the flanks of her defensive chain. It is, of course, an axiom of conquest that each time you advance you are creating a future need for a further advance to protect your new position. Nevertheless, Japan hoped that by her concerted campaigns she could drive her enemies back to such a distance that she would be able to halt her forces on natural defensive lines.

This she has not been able to do. The United Nations still hold bases on and from which it is possible for them to organize and launch striking forces to attack the Japanese positions, both new and old. These will be used—amply and effectively—as the war progresses.

And finally, it must be considered a weakness of the Japanese defensive ring that communications and transport must be carried on very largely by water. As we have seen only too clearly here at home, sea-borne communications are extremely vulnerable to attack. At worst they may be cut, at best they compel the defensive country to divert much of her naval strength to convoy and antisubmarine patrol. Japan is not a country which can replace her shipping losses easily, and it may well turn out that the steady attrition of her shipping, both mercantile and naval, may play a considerable part in her ultimate defeat.

But let me emphasize once again that these weaknesses will certainly not of themselves cause Japan to be defeated. They must be exploited— taken advantage of—by determined aggressive action by the United Nations. The strength of the Japanese people lies in their fanatical obedience to authority. The great strength of the American people lies in their ability to think and act for themselves, without waiting for orders from above. Our fathers tamed a continent without waiting for someone to tell them how to do it. It took no directive from the High Command to call the Minute Men from their plows to battle. We ourselves can do no less. Let us not wait for our Government to do all our thinking for us. Our leaders in Washington already bear an immense burden. Let us not add to it by expecting them to lead us by the hand every step of the road to victory.

Let us remember one thing—it is *our* war.

5

Why We Can No Longer Do Business with Japan

JAPAN IS fighting counter to her own welfare and prosperity.

Let us go back a little. Diplomacy is often associated in the minds of the public with the thought of appeasement. "Appeasement" is a much-used—mostly misused—term that gives rise to many misconceptions, especially as it conjures up the picture of Munich and what happened there and afterward. For several years during the middle and late 30's our Government endeavored to avoid antagonizing Japan, notwithstanding the fact that Japan had done a great deal to antagonize us. We do not believe in war, we did not want war, we thought wars should be avoided, and at that time we were in no respect prepared for war. Economic pressures in the form of embargoes and other similar steps are a form of warfare and they definitely constitute threats. Now, one of the most fatal errors that can be made in diplomacy is to threaten when one is not in a position to back up one's threats, if need be, by force. To threaten and then to have to back down is fatal to a nation's influence. Action in accordance with this, whether it is labeled "appeasement" or any other term, is plain common sense. The President, in a published statement in July, 1942, made clear certain important aspects of that problem. During my years in Japan I constantly took the position that the application of economic pressure against Japan would inevitably start our relations on a downward course which might end in war, and that under no circumstances should we embark on such a course unless or until we were prepared to face eventual war. The time finally came when I felt it no longer desirable to follow a negative policy, and at that time I took the position that the question then at issue was not *whether* we must call a halt to Japan's plans of expansion but when—for the threat to American vital interests if that expansion should continue was of the gravest nature. Up until then, oil and scrap iron and other commodities had been flowing freely from our country to Japan, but at approximately that time our imposition of embargoes began; and that again seemed to me to be plain common sense, and in my opinion it was with clear manifestation of plain common sense and wisdom that our Government handled the then developing situation.

The term "appeasement" is, as I have indicated, open to misconceptions. I prefer the term "constructive conciliation," and during all the ten years of my mission to Japan I endeavored to follow a policy of constructive conciliation. That term connotes building, and no one is going to be foolish enough to try to build anything, if he wishes it to be of a permanent character, unless a solid foundation on which to build has first been laid. I constantly tried to lay such a foundation. At times and under certain Japanese governments I was optimistic of success. But these favorable periods proved to be but temporary and in every case such governments failed and were succeeded by Cabinets in tune with the military extremists. All during the summer of 1941 we were doing our very best to lay a solid foundation which would support and insure a structure of friendly relations with the Japanese Government. I constantly pointed out to the Japanese—and our Secretary of State, Mr. Hull, was doing the same—that they had everything to gain and nothing to lose by concluding

38

a reasonable agreement with us and that such an agreement would bring in its wake a return to a free flow of trade and commerce, financial co-operation, and free access to the raw materials of East Asia on a basis of equal opportunity, which would inevitably result in mutual advantage to our two countries, a rising standard of living in Japan, and assurance of future prosperity. These arguments fell on deaf ears. It was found utterly impossible to lay any solid foundation, and those who wanted and who worked to do that were rapidly overwhelmed by the military extremists and pro-Axis elements in the country. Thus the *effort* to reach an agreement and to preserve peace failed and war ensued.

During all this time our Government would not and did not connive at or give any assent to the aggressions which Japan had committed and was committing. But the United States *was* prepared to meet every evidence of good will on Japan's part. We were Japan's most powerful neighbor, and we wanted to be a *good* neighbor to Japan, if Japan herself would be a good neighbor to us, to China, and to the other countries in the Pacific.

We were prepared to offer the Japanese everything for which her leaders professed to be fighting. We offered them sound trade, on terms advantageous to both countries. We offered them the powerful financial co-operation of the United States toward putting their fiscal house in order. All that we asked was that Japan abandon her militarist aggressions, cease being a bad neighbor in East Asia, and enjoy with us the prosperity that we and they could have found in common. We did not, do not, and never shall assent to Japan's assuming the hegemony of the Far East as a robber and an aggressor.

The Japanese rejected assurance of the prosperity, the security, and the welfare for which they say that they are fighting. They attacked us. They added us to the list of those whom they seek to conquer and to despoil.

They attacked us because they did not want the prosperity of honest industry, fair trade, and sound finance. They did not want co-operation and peaceful international relations. The Japanese militarist wanted what their German allies miscall *Lebensraum*. Strange, is it not, that despite their already far-flung occupied territories and their intensive efforts to propagate a maximum increase in population, especially male population, the Japanese constantly harped on the theme that territorial expansion is necessary for their allegedly congested homeland? They say that they want a so-called Greater East Asia Co-Prosperity Sphere including the South Seas. We have seen—the people of Korea and Formosa, of Manchuria and of other parts of occupied China have seen with the bitter realism of experience, just as the people of Hong Kong and the Philippines, Indo-China, Thailand, the Malay States, Singapore, the Dutch East Indies, and many islands of the South Seas, are witnessing today—what that euphemism "Co-Prosperity Sphere" really stands for. The Japanese love slogans; one might almost say that they govern by slogans. Their "Holy War" in China is one such slogan. Co-Prosperity means quite simply, and reduced to its elemental connotation, economic, financial, military, political, absolute hegemony, and all that can be comprised and denoted by a single ugly word—"slavery."

This *Lebensraum* of the aggressor nations has nothing to do with room in which to live. It means in fact room for brutal conquest and ruthless exploitation. The militarists who had come to power were not interested in the welfare of the Japanese people. They were interested only in their dreams of aggression. They cared little about exporting goods, or achieving an international economic balance. They wanted to hoard the strategic materials of war and to achieve the unwholesome prosperity of unending armament.

As Japan militarized herself more and more, Japan had no surpluses to export. Domestic civilian production was cut to the bone. The materials for a fair and reciprocally beneficial exchange of goods were no longer there. Japan could export subversive agents, and spies, and saboteurs; Japan could export her invading armies; but Japan could not export these and at the same time have the goods with which to trade on a fair basis.

Hence the alleged necessity for *Lebensraum,* or special spheres, and for the whole structure of totalitarian economics. The Japanese militarists turned from one kind of economic system—the honest kind, based on a real exchange of goods, in which we and they had lived and dealt for more than eighty years—to another kind of economic system, devised and developed by their Axis partners in Europe. This other kind is fundamentally dishonest, since it requires that the conquering power import without exporting. The economics of totalitarianism is wholesale robbery. Since Japan has invaded China, the Japanese can no longer deal with the Chinese on equitable terms. Therefore, the Japanese must go into China and take and take and take from the Chinese without giving them anything of value in exchange.

Even the Japanese militarists could not continue indefinitely a program of outright larcenies and burglaries. The robbery is reduced to a system. They have made that system resemble finance. Like our finance, it deals with money. Like ours it uses the familiar terms of cash, credit, loans, stock companies, government subsidies, tariffs, taxes, and so on. Like ours, it tries to fit the habits by which all modern men think and work. There the resemblance ceases.

Our financial system supports a means of production designed to benefit both producers and consumers. Our public finance is intended to pay for government, to pay for the enlargement and maintenance of freedom, and to correct inequities in our economic life. Our international finance is a method of recording and facilitating the actual exchange of real goods and real services. We do not conceive of trade as flowing only one way. For many years, the reciprocal-trade-agreements policy of the United States has been a complete antithesis to the economics for which Japan and Germany now stand.

The Japanese people were not twisted from the one economic system to the other in a single night. The change was accomplished within Japan by the rising tide of military fanaticism. The Japanese people have strong traces of zealotry and fanaticism in their individual and their national thinking, but they did not yield to their present totalitarianism without reluctance. They were seduced by their rulers—particularly by the military chauvinists—over a period of many years. It is terrible to consider the corruption of a people by its own leaders, its own government.

The Japanese leaders had to change the mind of the nation from the practical, simple terms of economics and welfare to the terms of a mythology of war. The Japanese fight because of ancient dreams and traditional ambitions which they are unable to shake off. They are not bad financiers engaging incidentally in a war; they are military fanatics to whom the power and the glory of conquest appeals far more than the accumulating economic values and the general welfare of peace.

In 1930, Japan was still a constitutional empire operating on the basis of accepted economic standards and setting a pace for progress which was almost unmatched elsewhere in the world. A succession of civilian governments had promised Japan peace. The naval treaties had assured Japan permanent defensive security in the Pacific, and had made it possible for her people to avoid the ruinous expense of a naval race with us and with Great Britain.

The turning point in 1931, precipitated by the attack of the Japanese Army on Manchuria, ushered in a campaign which was directed as much against the Japanese people as against the rest of the world. Relying on a fabricated and falsified incident, the Imperial Japanese Army conquered Manchuria without consulting the electorate, or the Parliament, or the Cabinet, or the Foreign Office. This action jeopardized the international position of Japan. As Japanese traditionalists, even the strongest industrialists and financiers were powerless to restrict the growth and the operations of the Army. Army budgets continued to rise; Army power grew.

The Japanese invasion of Manchuria eleven years ago, which Tokyo officialdom explained to the world as an economic and strategic necessity, at once led to an alienation of Japan's best customers—China and America—and to a subversion of the domestic business system of Japan.

That this invasion was not economic in its objective is shown by the fact that the Japanese military authorities in Manchuria tried to set up a curious sort of army socialism. They were not interested in the welfare of the Chinese whom they had conquered. They were not even interested in profits for Japanese capital or increased wages of Japanese labor. They concerned themselves only with the procuring and supplying of further materials of war for the Imperial Japanese Army.

In other words, they made war in order to acquire more weapons with which to make more war. The *Lebensraum,* the so-called East Asia sphere, which began to be talked about at this time, is not an economic concept. It is a concept of conquest. Japan could have traded freely with us, with China, with all the nations of the world. Generally speaking, she was doing so. The Japanese extremists did not want to trade—because Japan's military leaders realized that, for war purposes, Japan had to become autarchic. The history of Japan from 1932 is the history of increasing and multiplying controls.

During those years, I saw the Japanese generals follow policies not unlike those of Hitler in Europe. Trade was cartelized. Foreign enterprises were tied in with the domestic war economy. Foreign exchange became the subject of repressive regulation. By the spring of 1938 an Emergency Capital Adjustment Law had tied down every ordinary act of commerce to the military-resources plan.

There was no time in all these years when the Japanese Army actually said to their people, "We shall fight America and Britain." Pamphleteers and journalists discussed that possibility; statesmen hinted at it. But the issue was never brought to a focus. The Japanese Army and leaders called for more expansion in China, magnified every instance of Chinese resentment or resistance into evidence of conspiracy or recalcitrancy, and kept the Japanese Empire alert with the clamor of war. They never let this ultimate issue become clear. Japanese themselves, they realized that their people had no choice but to follow them, provided the process of militarization was not too rapid.

Let me give you a few instances of what happened to the people in Japan during those years.

Japanese big business was cajoled, bribed, or blackmailed into self-regimentation and into acquiescence to government control. When I arrived in Japan in 1932, Japanese business was still a model of comparative efficiency, drive, and inventiveness. By 1941, it had become an adjunct to the military regime. Japanese investors were driven more and more into government investment. Their overseas holdings were jeopardized by the irresponsible actions of their government. Investment in the much-touted occupied areas in China was on the Army's terms and was subject to the corrupt exactions of the puppet governments under the Japanese Army.

Far more important, Japanese farmers continued their accumulation of debt. Their poverty made possible the cheap food of the cities. Their misery drove their sons and daughters into the factories to serve for the lowest wages in a modernized state. The wretchedness of the Japanese farmer, his low standard of living, has been the keystone of Japanese international competition. The China war did nothing—either in the Manchuria phase or in later phases—to help the Japanese farmer. His sons died in it. He was taxed for it. Occasional food shortages gave him the illusion of prosperity, when he sold his products on a rising market—but the Japanese farmer remains the first and the constant victim of Japanese militarism.

Between the investors and the farmers, the middle classes were driven into an insecurity which would only be relieved by state control. Their freedom of movement, of thought, of expression, was circumscribed artfully by appeals to their patriotism or their superstition, or both. Their savings were solicited for Japanese Government loans which were secured by the slender chance of Japan's winning some sort of victory and then stopping and consolidating her gains.

With developments such as these, two seemingly incompatible tendencies were produced. Japan was going bankrupt. Japan was getting stronger. The two changes were actually part of the same pattern. Japan was departing from a free economic system based upon the domestic and foreign exchange of goods and services over to an unfree economy based on the domestic destruction of goods in military enterprises and supported by the foreign expropriation of goods.

Once new territory was acquired, the Japanese invaders alienated the conquered people by uncouth, cruel, or atrocious behavior. They installed traitorous, renegade, indigenous local leaders as puppet rulers. They built up a currency system that rested on the fiat of the Japanese Army and issued bank notes payable only in death to anyone who did not honor them. With this currency, the Japanese military manipulated exchange so as to conduct trade on a ruthlessly unfair basis. They supplemented this with outright confiscation, or capital levies, or simply with the murder of the property owners and the enslavement of the workers. Japanese-run monopolies fixed prices on what their own people wanted at ridiculously low levels, and Japanese military patrols "bought" at these prices. On this basis Japan was able to develop a flourishing flow into Japan of goods, until the occupied area was pumped dry. Then some concessions would be made, in an attempt to prime the pump and sink it deeper into the well.

By the standards of past European imperialism, this kind of development is not imperialism. It is stark international holdup. Nevertheless, it worked, and it is still working, and it will continue to supply Japan with materials until we go in and stop the flow with bullets, bombs, and torpedoes.

Japan is finished and ruined in terms of *honest* finance. Her trade is discredited. Her foreign investments are held only at the points of bayonets. Her customers are completely alienated.

Nevertheless, in terms of *dishonest* finance, Japan flourishes. Japan has —with her temporary conquests—all the raw materials needed by a great power. She has at her command almost limitless labor supplies. She does not have any friendly rivals in the regions that her armed forces control. Her industrial potential is relatively high and efficient. Labor and the

46

farmers are quiet. At the moment, all this power is pouring into the military economy behind the Japanese fleets, armies, and air forces.

We face this formidable enemy. Our Japanese antagonists live far more cheaply than we do. They conserve their goods. They do not worry about their victims. They concentrate everything on winning the war.

The United Nations will not do business with military Japan again. After the years I have spent attempting to safeguard a free American economy against the potential workings of a Japanese military economy, I am relieved to think that we shall never try again to preserve the peace and our rights by dealing with a Japan which pursues the course of a robber state. The financial system that Japan has created is one that violates all concepts of honest dealing—irrespective of the particular epoch or system. It is the mere mask for a predatory military oligarchy which neither comprehends nor approves the principles of honest exchange, of stable money, and of international good faith.

The basic issues of this war are political; they transcend considerations of national financial or economic interest; the economic systems of the United Nations, whatever they may be, can be reconciled—each one with each of the others—so long as they proceed on the principles of the Atlantic Charter and the subsequent pronouncements of our United Nations leaders.

The war finance of the United States, of Britain, of China, and of other United Nations differ one from another, but they are separated collectively from Axis finance by an unbridgeable gulf. We have a system of free enterprise, which has grown and has become modified by economic and military necessity over the years. Britain has an economy substantially little different from our own. China is committed by both theory and

47

practice to a joint state and individualist economy, according to Sun Yat-
sen's principle of popular prosperity.

These systems are all in contradiction to the philosophies of aggression
nurtured by Japanese and German militarism. The Axis powers have attacked. They think—they may not be as sure now as they were nine
months ago—that they will win. We *know* that *we* will win, and bring
freedom—not omitting the basic, practical freedom from want—to all
mankind.

I should like to emphasize certain memorable statements made recently
by the Secretary and the Under Secretary of State. In his broadcast of July
23, 1942, the Secretary began: "The conflict now raging throughout the
earth is not a war of nation against nation. It is not a local or regional war
or even a series of such wars. . . . On our side . . . we are united in our
determination to destroy the world-wide forces of ruthless conquest and
brutal enslavement. Their defeat will restore freedom or the opportunity for freedom alike to all countries and all peoples." In his address at
the Arlington National Amphitheater on Memorial Day, May 30, 1942,
the Under Secretary of State declared simply and categorically, "The age
of imperialism is ended." In that same address he adumbrated the cre-
ative task of United Nations finance, both public and private, in the postwar world, in which we shall aid our invaded allies—Russia, China, and
the other European and Asiatic peoples—to rebuild their homelands. He
said:

The problem which will confront us when the years of the
postwar period are reached is not primarily one of production.
For the world can readily produce what mankind requires. The
problem is rather one of distribution and purchasing power; of

48

providing the mechanism whereby what the world produces may be fairly distributed among the nations of the world; and of providing the means whereby the people of the world may obtain the world's goods and services.

This is the task we face: to assure and safeguard our victory for the ages, so that no nation may be led into madness again, as Japan has been led, and no exploiters can again organize any nation into a marauding horde bent on conquering, plundering, and ruling over other nations. Japan had prepared for this war for years. Providence has equipped us for the winning of it for centuries.

6

Japanese Youth

IN THE years when the Western world was hopeful of lasting peace and bent upon preserving that peace through disarmament, economic agreements, and the cultivating of international friendships, it was a common sight in Japan—and a startling one to recently arrived Americans—to see little fellows scarcely big enough to walk togged out in military caps and playing military games. Anyone who passed a schoolyard would be even more startled to hear the blood-curdling yells coming from the throats of twelve-year-old boys as they charged across a field with real guns and bayonets, and in a manner so realistic as to be chilling.

If the visitor stayed long enough, he would soon come to realize that for Japan the years of peace were but years of preparation, and that from early childhood Japanese children were being reared for war, and reared with the thought that their greatest good fortune would be to die on the field of battle.

Military drill and maneuvers play an important part in Japan's educational system. In primary schools the way is prepared by marching, exercise, and indoctrination in the theory of the invincible and militant state. Then come regular military drill under officers of the Japanese Army, week-end trips to Army camps, and long marches with Army packs in order to build up endurance. These military activities have priority over all academic work in Japanese colleges. When the Army decides to send a group of students out on maneuvers, classes are canceled.

Recently the Tokyo radio itself admitted that fourteen-year-old boys were being drafted as seamen. "Thus," it was announced, "the structure of victory will be prepared." The same radio has told how youngsters are being trained in the operation of tanks.

Japan's young men have been trained for years toward one specific end—making war. That they have been well trained to that end has been made abundantly clear by their brilliant military successes since Pearl Harbor—successes which it will do us no good to minimize.

In Japan the training of youth for war is not simply military training. It is a shaping—a warping, if you will—of the mind of youth from the earliest years. Every Japanese school child on national holidays goes to his school and takes part in a ritual intended to impress on him his duties to the state and to the Emperor. Several times each year every child is taken with the rest of his schoolmates to a place where the spirits of dead soldiers are enshrined. The military aspect of the state is, and has been for many years, stressed above all other functions of government. Of the state's duty to the individual, or of individual rights and liberties, the Japanese youth hears nothing. Of his obligation to serve the state, especially through military service, he hears every day.

If despite this indoctrination a young man has enough intellectual perseverance to study the ways of other governments and to speak in their favor, he may find himself in a prison cell, and subjected to torture until he makes a false confession or dies of mistreatment. Such cases were frequent in the thirties and were well known despite a rigid censorship.

The whole concept of Japanese education has been built upon the military formula of obeying commands. The spirit of free inquiry and intel-

51

ligent criticism that we consider fundamental to education is not encouraged in Japan. It is the student's duty to receive without question what
the professor provides and to hand it back at examination time.

This attitude in education stems from the idea of paternal authority in
the family and in the state. For Japan has seized upon the authority of the
family system, with its deference to the head of the house, and has taught
its people to revere the authority of the Emperor on a national plane as
the father of the household is honored and obeyed within the home.

Thus a Japanese youngster—who is born, we may assume, with the
same basic desire for self-expression and self-fulfillment that any child
possesses—soon finds himself hedged round with powerful authorities
whom he must not disobey. Within the family he must defer to his father
and older brothers. At school he discovers not only that he must obey the
teacher, but also that the power of the group is invoked against him if he
steps out of line. Japanese school children are taught to exert group pressure on any member who is unique or different. Thus through ridicule
or threats the youngster learns the power of the group and the discomfort
of which awaits him if he asserts his individual desire over the collective
will.

In the period of the 1920's there was, indeed, a fad among youth for the
unheroic pleasures of modern life. Young men and women turned to
dancing, the cinema, free criticism, modernistic writing; many of them
worshiped all things up-to-date and Western, whether good or bad. But
the *mobo* and *mogo*—Japanese nicknames based on the English "modern boy" and "modern girl"—were repressed by police and propaganda.
The harmless if stupid pleasures of these adolescents were portrayed as
living sedition of *Kokutai,* the special and awful body politic of Japan.

The drab, universal discipline closed down on them, and an insular puritanism made sure that Japanese youth conformed to the heroic.

Group pressure in order to make the individual conform is exerted not only through the school and through military training, but also through so-called youth groups which further indoctrinate the young in the concept of the supremacy of the state.

Perhaps the most notorious of these is the Japan Young Men's Federation, a reactionary group claiming five million members and headed by the notorious Colonel Hashimoto, the man who commanded the shore fire against the British gunboat *Ladybird*. Recent information from Japan tells of a new over-all association which will consolidate all youth organizations and regiment them along nationalistic lines.

It may not be out of place here to mention Japan's efforts to Japanize the conquered territories by imposing youth societies upon them. Japan, which has had singularly great success in preaching the nationalistic faith to its own youth within a few generations, is hopeful of converting all Asia, through the corruption of its youth, in the years that lie ahead.

In the Philippines, the Boy Scouts and Girl Scouts, with their principles of self-reliance and initiative, are being replaced by organizations designed to propagate the superiority of Japan and its divine right to rule. In the puppet state of Manchuria, Japan is regimenting the youth in order to obtain a badly needed labor force. Six hundred thousand youths will be assigned to what is called "patriotic labor service." Tokyo boasts that they will be treated like an army. "No person who fails to take part in the service can be considered a full-fledged citizen" is Tokyo's ominous threat. In North China, too, an association to "guide" the youth of the country has gone into operation.

Those who are aware of the effect of Hitler's grip on the youth of Germany will have some idea of what Japan plans for Asia and has already done to its own youth. The Japanese soldier is the result of calculated, continuous indoctrination in the glories of the militarist state. His willingness to sacrifice himself on the battlefield is not a result of intellectual commitment to a cause. It is the product of a far more dangerous training of his emotions from childhood to respond to the appeal of sacrifice for the state. All the forces which have produced him—the family, the school, compulsory military service, state religion, and the compulsive power of the group over the individual—have shaped him to this end. Unquestioning obedience and self-sacrifice are his creed—obedience and sacrifice to the militaristic state.

A concept of life in which the individual is merely an unimportant and expendable appendage of the state will not and cannot prevail. But to defeat it we must become as tough, as willing to make sacrifices, as the Japanese themselves. Our vision of youth is something different and something worth fighting for. As our President expressed it in his address to the International Students' Assembly:

"The cause of the United Nations is the cause of youth itself. It is the hope of the new generation and the generations that are to come; hope for a new life that can be lived in freedom, in justice and decency."

7

Truth in Japan

IF THERE is one thing a militaristic government fears, it is that its people may learn the truth. There has been in Japan for many years now the most rigid control over every medium of expression. All radio stations and programs are under government control. Books cannot be published until they have been registered with the authorities. Imported books and periodicals have been carefully scrutinized and refused admission if they contained anything that was thought to endanger belief in the mythology on which the Japanese have been raised or to encourage resistance to the militaristic rulers.

To understand how the Japanese people have been misled and misinformed, it is sufficient to look at two governmental activities—the control of the press with respect to war information, and the campaign for what the Japanese quite frankly label "thought control."

While it is true that the Japanese are a news-minded people and their newspapers—with regard to physical plant and circulation—quite unequaled in the Orient, they have been consistently misinformed. They have never been told the truth regarding their losses in China during the past ten years, for their government has allowed only the smallest fraction of casualties to be announced. The Japanese Government has never admitted a real defeat in all its long course of conquest and aggression dur-

55

ing the past eleven years. It has described every defeat as "a withdrawal according to plan, after the achievement of planned objectives."

Such deliberate misinformation reveals a fatal flaw in Japanese civilization—the fear of criticism. A government can remain healthy only so long as it is subjected to the criticism of its citizens. In Japan criticism of the state has always been dangerous. No other nation in modern times has witnessed so many political assassinations. And almost invariably the victims have been eminent men who dared to criticize the chauvinists.

Another reason for the rigid suppression of criticism is the myth of invincibility. The Japanese Army has encouraged the fiction that it is invincible. Perhaps the cultivation of such an attitude hides a basic fear, for it is the weak, not the strong, who dare not acknowledge failure.

Yet the people of Japan have not been entirely fooled by the refusal of their leaders to tell the truth about their losses in China. They have seen the return of the white boxes containing the ashes of their dead. They have seen the maimed and the wounded. They know that casualties have been far in excess of admitted losses.

Meanwhile they have been fed such a rich diet of alleged victories that victory has lost its savor. For eleven years they have had nothing but victories in their news—victories that have made many of them skeptical of the worth of victory. It was the realization of this skepticism which recently led the government to send back from the occupied territories token shipments of food or rubber or some other commodity in order to convince the people that some material benefit was accruing to them from the sacrifice of their fathers, husbands, and sons. Such a policy, however, has not satisfied the millions who depended upon foreign trade for their livelihood—the silk growers, the makers of rayon and pottery and a hundred other things for which Japan now has no market. Nor has it explained to the Japanese people why the China war, which the militarists promised to end within a few weeks, has dragged on for many years without a settlement.

No hint of Japan's massacre of Chinese civilians has been allowed to reach the Japanese people, so far as their censors have been able to prevent it. No word of the atrocities committed at Nanking appeared in Japanese newspapers. The strictest censorship was also exercised over outside sources that might have introduced the news into Japan. Magazines from America that exposed that horrible story were clipped before being sent on to subscribers.

When Japan suffered heavy naval losses in the battle of Midway, the Japanese radio followed its usual formula and described the fight as a great victory for Japan. When Japanese forces landed on the Aleutian Islands, the operation was described as one which had put an end to America's hopes of resistance. The Japanese people have not been told of the American operations in the Aleutians which resulted in the withdrawal of their forces from the smaller islands near Kiska. They have not been informed of the retreat in New Guinea, or of their heavy naval losses.

Yet far more serious than the withholding of all unfavorable military news is the ban on any information that might raise a doubt regarding the national mythology. Because they are taught that they descend from the gods, the Japanese are not allowed to know the scientific and historical truth of their racial origins. They are led to believe—and many do believe it—that they are different from all the rest of the world. Just the other day a broadcast from Japan intended for Japanese ears announced: "Japan is a nation made by gods. Japan is a mother nation, and those who are born in Japan are born of God. We are the greatest people in the world."

They are regaled with such preposterous transformations of history as the following: "Ancient Japan ruled the Asiatic continent and handed down a great cultural tradition. . . . Japan performed tremendous historical accomplishments not only in China but also in India, Arabia, Central Asia, Siberia, etc., in the guise of Ural-Altaic or Indian peoples." This is comparable to the German claim that every great man in all history had a German streak in him somewhere; the Japanese are no more like the Indians than are we.

Such maunderings may seem to us so ridiculous as to be trivial. But they are not trivial. They have so poisoned the mind of a nation that only complete and final military defeat will convince the Japanese people of its falsehood. Fanaticism has been built up by crafty and calculating leaders with but one end in view—to make the Japanese people a fighting machine with no regard for individual rights or individual safety, and with only one thought—to fight on to death for the glory of the state.

The creation of this attitude has for the most part taken place within the last fifty years, although the Japanese have preached its ancient origins so persuasively that even in America we have come to believe that it is a thing of long standing. By careful supervision of all education and the means of communication, by strict police surveillance over every meeting and indeed over every individual, the leaders of Japan have within the short space of half a century built a powerful fighting machine upon the ignorance of their own people. Literacy has been encouraged, but only so far as to make the populace susceptible to a strictly controlled press and to the flood of nationalistic propaganda. Education has been made compulsory, but only to indoctrinate the youth of the land with the proposition that it is Japan's right to rule the world, and to train them in the arts of war.

Literacy and education have been not for truth, but for deception; not for freedom, but for slavery to the militaristic state; not for happiness, but for privation; not for the fostering of universal humanity, but for the doctrine of racial superiority.

Such a state can fear nothing more than that its people shall learn the truth. Such a state must, as Japan has done, imprison those who attempt political reforms, persecute those teachers who will not be bound by half truth or misinterpretation in science and history, suppress all news of defeat or loss of the armed forces, and attempt to ring the minds of the people within a charmed circle of fairy tales.

That all this has been done in so short a space of time gives us at least the hope that once Japan's leaders have been thoroughly defeated and discredited, an equal transformation in the interests of truth, and for the welfare of the Japanese as well as the world at large, may be brought about.

8

Is This a Racial War?

IN THE midst of this tragic, world-wide devastation, it is heartening to look at the record of our own nation. By ideal standards, it has not been irreproachable. We have done some foolish, selfish, or offensive things. But by contrast with the record of our enemies, our own record has lived up to Bryant's characterization of Lincoln:

> . . . *slow to smite and swift to spare,*
> *Gentle and merciful and just!*

As an American, I am proud of this. I am glad that we have not purchased mean and temporary military advantages at the price of national dishonor. I am glad that we have not played a part in international politics so cold, so calculating, and so inhumanly selfish that our posterity faces dishonor before mankind. I am glad that we entered the ordeal through which we are now passing as the victims and not as the makers of war. We have stabbed no nation in the back. We have not murderously assaulted a neighbor. We came to the brink of war cleanly and honorably. The Japanese Government and people had at all times before them a clear statement of the intentions of the American Government. These intentions were peaceful, fair, and sincere. Our Government could have formulated no other kind of policy. Our people, who are enlightened, could have supported no other kind of policy.

What would the American people have done if an American government, in the midst of diplomatic conversations, had attacked another country wantonly and without notice? Would not our people have raised a clamor against such a government? In any event, would not large minorities—if not the majority—have criticized, sabotaged, or even revolted against such a policy of aggression and treachery? And—to reveal the hypothesis in all its absurdity—could the American people in the first place have elected a government capable of conceiving such a deed?

You and I know the answers to these questions. America today is trusted by her allies, because she is worthy of trust. That trust does not rest on the fiat of a few leaders. It rests on the humane, peaceful outlook of the people who elect the leaders, and on the democracy which makes all leaders responsible to the people. In the broadest sense, we are constitutionally incapable of aggression.

How, then, did the Japanese people turn aside from the ways of peace? Are they not a cultured people? Are they not industrious and literate and possessed of high standards of morality and decency? They are all this, but they have forgotten the teachings of the Buddhist and Confucian sages from whom they are supposed to have learned, teachings which in our tongue have been expressed by Emerson: "The true test of civilization is, not the census, not the size of cities, nor the crops—no, but the kind of man the country turns out." The Japanese people have been led downward and away from civilization. The leaders of Japan have promoted a militarism—an ideology of vain conquest—which has seduced their own susceptible people. They have *de*civilized the purposes and ideals of modern life, while leaving untouched the tremendous benefits of technical, military, and political potentialities of modernism.

You will all agree that as a human problem, it appears difficult to understand how proud, modern, well-trained people like the Japanese and the Germans can be led to crime and slaughter—not only be led, but go willingly. They saw the value of peace and the awful risks of war. But they went to war then, and they fight *now,* for the sake of more war—for the autarchy, the hegemony over whole continents, the arbitrary command of man power and materials, which will enable them to fight further wars. And when they are asked why the dishonor, why the suffering, the death, the terrible waste, they answer, "It is the destiny of our race."

Race! The Japanese, whose national origins are and probably always will be a subject of dispute but who certainly comprise within the boundaries of the designation the "Yamato race" a variety of strains and types, have proclaimed themselves not only a race but a superior, a divinely appointed race. They have taken as their agreed-upon forebears the Yamato people, who were still savages at about the time of Christ, when Han China had already produced on the continent opposite them a brilliant and luxurious civilization. They have woven the totemism and animism of simple-minded barbarians into a terrifying cult of a god which is Japan, and have designated themselves the true humans—the offspring of the sole and original god who is exemplified by the sun. The religion thus developed is far from the simple, devout sects of Shinto which survived in medieval and early modern Japan among austere, patriotic men. This modern cult of racial superiority is an affront to the rulers it presumes to honor and to the nation which is gullible enough to accept it. This cult escapes almost altogether from the religious, indeed, and becomes coldly political—the propaganda instrument of a ruthless and ambitious military machine.

The Japanese talk of their racial war. They declare Chiang Kai-shek a European in spirit, because they hate him, just as the Nazis allow the

Japanese to think of themselves as Aryan, if they wish. The uttermost disgusting absurdity of this Japanese racialism was reached, perhaps, by the enactment of anti-Semitic laws by Japan and the puppets of Manchukuo, so-called.

Like the German militarists, the Japanese chauvinists saw that they could not teach modern men to die for economic reasons, because the men who die—even the men who fight—do not profit by the economics of aggressive war.

The Japanese militarists could not lead their people into a religious war, because religion has created its own foundation of good will throughout the world today; it is, we hope, almost impossible for sincere men of different religions to fight because of their religions.

The Japanese militarists could not persuade their people to fight for the old shibboleths of power politics—of the grandeur of empire simply as empire, of *Realpolitik* for its own sake. That myth died at Versailles. I saw it die. At the time we knew that something great and evil had been driven out of the world; we did not know how much evil remained.

The Japanese militarists, like the Germans, could not appeal to war for the sake of booty, or for religion, or for old-fashioned national ambitions. They turned to racialism. *Race* sounded scientific.

They had an attentive and docile audience. The Japanese language is peculiar. Few of Japan's neighbors show clear evidence of blood kinship with Japan. The ancient myths about Japan's Divine Empire were at hand, ready to be recast into the pseudo-scientific terms of metropolitan men. The Japanese race was singled out as *the* Master People of the entire world. The ancient sagas of Japan were twisted into this modern propaganda.

We Americans know that "Oriental," or "Asiatic," or "yellow" *races* exist only as suppositions. We know that our scientists have been infinitely more careful in their definition of race. We know what crimes the Germans have committed in the name of an Aryanism and a Semitism which never existed. Nevertheless, we have gone on day after day using the terms ourselves. Our press refers to the Japanese as "Asiatics," and forgets that Japan makes China her first and greatest enemy.

The preposterous myth of the "rising tide of color" has aided and abetted the growth of Fascism and National Socialism. Now the great racialist Hitler is helping the racialist Japanese leaders in the vain attempt to persuade the rest of the world that this nightmare alarm is an historical truth. *Both* champions of this concept of a long-prophesied racial conflict are today allied in making war against all free men.

To China the world owes an eternal debt of gratitude for destroying a myth which holds infinite danger for the future of the human race—the myth that there is some deep-rooted antagonism between the Western and Eastern peoples and that this antagonism can be resolved only by one or the other conquering and enslaving its rival. It is a myth which has appeared under different names at different times. As a myth of Nordic solidarity, it has been busily fostered in some Occidental countries by reactionaries who have sought to use this alleged peril as a mask to hide their own designs. In the Far East it has appeared in different shape. There Japan calls it the Pan-Asia movement and pretends that she is leading a crusade on behalf of the peoples of Asia. In either shape it is a fraud, an attempt to hide designs of aggression behind screens of prejudice and hatred. And China, free China, one of the great Eastern peoples standing boldly against aggression, has demonstrated the falsity of this. Today we can see clearly that love of freedom and the will to fight for it are not the exclusive heritage of any nation or any race. Today we see European Germany and Italy allied with Far Eastern Japan against a common front of United Nations prominent among which are the Asiatic peoples of China and the Philippines.

And this fact holds in itself tremendous possibilities for the future of the world.

The Japanese have preached the racialism of their own utter superiority to the rest of mankind, and have also preached the racialism of all Asia against the Western peoples. They contradict the second with the first. The horrors which have been inflicted by Nazi Germans on Jewish Europeans today are equaled by Japanese cruelty and arrogance toward other and neighboring Asiatic peoples. The Japanese have made enemies of the peoples whom they profess to lead in a crusade. This came because of their unbearable attitude of superiority and because of the violence and unfairness which are always resorted to by those who seek to bolster up such pretensions to superiority.

The Japanese fight to make themselves superior in Asia, and then to make Asiatics supreme throughout the world; but they forget that the other peoples of Asia do not covet the doubtful glory of being Japan's creatures and are little concerned about the claims to or aspiration for racial superiority. What the peoples of Asia want—the peoples of China, of India, of Western Asia, all of them—are the real freedoms: freedom of speech, freedom of religion, freedom from want, and freedom from fear.

Our allies: the Filipinos on Bataan; the heroic Indonesians, who stood loyal to the Netherlands; the Chinese, who with rifles have withstood Japan's tanks and planes—these men, and others like them, can ultimately break the spirit and the will to fight of Japan. The Japanese myth of race will retain to the last its full bitter persuasiveness against us, but it will be vulnerable to the attacks of its presumed beneficiaries. We can challenge

Japan at a vulnerable point by showing contempt for doctrines and practices of racial conflict, by loyal co-operation with our allies in Asia, and by recognizing the human worth of peoples of other than the majority race within our own territories.

Now is the time, and this the battle, wherein we can show ourselves qualified for leadership. We can do one thing above all others.

To reach the basis of Japanese fanaticism we can and must give the lie to his racial pretensions and demonstrate that we accept freely and willingly the collaboration of the free and growing peoples of Asia. We must fight and we must show that we are fighting for world-wide peace and prosperity. We are confronted with the challenge of a global war. To meet this challenge we must have and we must cultivate the concept of a global unity of freedom: our Four Freedoms for all men and all nations.

9

Our Allies in the Pacific

U NITED NATIONS solidarity is a prelude to victory. For we must
not harbor the illusion that any one of us might be powerful
enough to defeat *this* enemy singlehanded. Nothing less than the combined wealth and strength and will power and effort of all the United
Nations will prevail.

Our allies have shown us that the spontaneous solidarity of free peoples can be a flexible and finely tempered weapon. The British, a
people wholly dedicated to a common purpose, will tell you that their
democracy is more alive today than ever before. When France fell in that
tragic June of 1940, Britain, with her Dominions, stood alone against the
Nazis and Fascists of Europe. The war might have ended at that moment.
Nothing but a miracle, it seemed, could save Britain from being overrun
by the Nazi hordes massed within twenty miles of her shores. But a miracle did save her. It was the miracle of the people to whom nothing mat-
tered but first to defend themselves and then to fight on to victory. They
forgot their rights—they thought only of their duties and their capacities.
They worked as they had never worked before, to replace the equipment
lost in France. They labored night and day on the defenses of their island.
Barbed wire and pill boxes appeared as if by magic on the cliffs and
beaches; antiaircraft guns and fighter planes came rolling off the factory

assembly lines; Home Guard volunteers loaded their old shotguns and drilled through the long summer evenings on the village greens. There was no need to talk of morale—no need to ask for volunteers, no need to persuade the people into making necessary sacrifices—for the things that had to be done no longer seemed like sacrifices. We owe much to the British Navy and Air Force. They stood, they held, between the Nazis and us and the rest of the Western Hemisphere—even the rest of the world. To the British people our debt is incalculable.

We can look with no less appreciation to our Russian allies to see the power of spontaneous solidarity. The Soviet people have proved that the best-trained military machine will falter and stop in the face of sheer courage and unwavering determination. Since their land was invaded, nothing else matters to the Soviet people but to work and fight and avenge their dead comrades. That determination fills their lives. It leaves no room for internal dissensions or personal ambitions, or indeed for any consideration of personal interests.

Now I ask you to give especial thought to the Chinese—our leading ally in the Pacific.

The thirty-first anniversary of the Chinese Republic, October 10, 1942, marked a milestone on a road of determined independence, exalted courage, insuperable staying power, and magnificent valor—the same sort of staying power and valor that brought George Washington through the dark days of Valley Forge to Yorktown and Foch from the Marne to Compiègne—the staying power and valor that will carry our heroic ally, China, under the superb leadership of Generalissimo Chiang Kai-shek, from the bridge at Luk'ouchiao to final victory.

On this anniversary we saluted the Chinese Republic and her leader with the deep affection of a sister republic, with great admiration and with profound respect. No reverses on the field of battle could quench their indomitable spirit, no seas of disaster were too deep for them to pass through unbroken, no destruction by fire and bomb could subdue or weaken their determination to survive and their will to win. Such nations, such people, and such leaders *cannot be defeated*.

The Pacific war is and will be a hard war. Our Chinese allies, who have held tenaciously to their own humane culture, are going to have to depend on us for technical and industrial assistance in various fields which they have not yet developed. Supplying both the Chinese forces and our own, we shall have to cross oceans and seas, mountains, valleys, and plains, to come to grips with Japanese militarism and destroy it at its roots.

The Pacific and the Far East, when we have cleared them of the scourge of war, will justify the effort and the sacrifices involved in that achievement. We, and the nations in that area that are resisting militarism and aggression, are fighting not only for freedom but also for world peace, world democracy, and world prosperity. Beyond the general aims of our war for survival there are positive high objectives in the Pacific and the Far East to which we can and shall attain.

First, once Japan is destroyed as an aggressive force, we know of no other challenging power that can appear in the Pacific. The nations now members of the Pacific Council in Washington are quite simply fighting primarily for freedom—to live their own national and individual lives, and to let live. No one of these powers has serious strategic claims or designs upon the independence or territory of another. There are no frontiers stained with centuries of the bloodshed of international war. The Pacific nations have clear geographical limits, sufficient natural resources, and a proved disposition to co-operate. Once militant Japan is out of the picture, there should remain no threat of further war in the Pacific area.

Japan is the one enemy, and the only enemy, of the peaceful peoples whose shores overlook the Pacific Ocean.

Second, the winning of the war will bring its own rewards in uniting the Pacific peoples. Friendships and opportunities for mutual education and enrichment, both material and spiritual, possess limitless possibilities for good. The share of the Chinese in the new Pacific is bound to be a great one.

Third, we can hold out the hope of a liberated Japan. A population as great as that of the German Reich waits to be freed not only from its militarist masters, but also from itself. The Japanese have great cultural assets with which they could continue to contribute to the happiness and civilization of mankind. But they have—particularly in recent years—been led along a road of militarism and overweening extremist ambition which have directed Japanese civilization into a blind alley of potential ruin. We and our allies of the United Nations can free those people of Japan who yearn in secret merely to be allowed to pursue their normal beauty-loving lives in peace, in their own homes, and in their own cultural surroundings. But we must realize that the captivity in which they are held is no mere temporary phenomenon of an occupying force or of a police control suddenly grown tyrannical: it is the despotism of tradition through the centuries—grown corrupt, savage, and untrue even to its own followers. Whatever desire some of the more enlightened elder statesmen of Japan may have had for peace, they have, as I have tried to make clear, in recent times been completely overridden by the utterly ruthless extremist elements in the country. Even during the period of our internment in Tokyo, the scorn in which they held the Foreign Office was only too evident, and whatever effort was made by the latter to bring our treatment into accord with international usage was in many cases arbitrarily overruled by the military and metropolitan police, who dealt with us in the Embassy not merely as prisoners but as though we were criminal prisoners.

In this, again, the role of China is of fundamental import—by reason of China's propinquity to Japan, by reason of China's cultural leadership of the Far East. For almost three thousand years, Chinese civilization has been the stabilizer and illuminator of Far Eastern life.

In the Pacific war we are, therefore, not only fighting for progress, for democracy, for the Four Freedoms of the Atlantic Charter. We are fighting to free the richest cultural heritage of East Asia, and in this fight we are proud of our indispensable ally, China, and of her leader, Generalissimo Chiang Kai-shek.

We must lay aside our prejudices and suspicions—inherited from the past—about our allies. For within the United Nations we are all on the same side; we are all fighting the same war against the same enemy and for the same survival and victory. It is absurd to discuss who is to help whom—to talk about "aid to China" or "aid to Russia." For in helping each other we are—every one of us—first, last, and always helping ourselves.

We had better dispense also with the luxury of thinking that we are somehow superior to the rest of the world, that we love freedom more; that we are more devoted to abstract principles of right and justice. My duties have taken me to the far corners of the earth, and my experience has proved—to me at least—that freedom and justice are no monopoly of ours but are the common aspirations of humanity wherever and whenever men and women have glimpsed these blessings.

10

Japan: the Pledge and the Performance

IT IS necessary that we now assess, coolly and impassively, the events of the past ninety years in the Pacific—the ninety years that have elapsed since Commodore Perry concluded with Japan the treaty that opened the way for the subsequent admission of Japan into the family of nations.

We are today being given dreadful evidence that the process of Japan's emergence from three centuries of isolation and of her assimilation into the family of nations is far from complete. Except for brief contacts at widely spaced intervals—the introduction into Japan of Chinese learning and arts in the seventh and twelfth centuries and the propagation of Roman Catholicism by Portuguese and Spanish priests in the sixteenth and seventeenth centuries—Japan had, for geographic and other reasons, been in virtual isolation since the very beginning of her history. Her civilization and culture had evolved, therefore, in a wholly self-contained environment. She had contributed nothing to the world at large and, notwithstanding superficial evidence to the contrary, she had remained, politically, socially, and intellectually, impervious to spasmodic foreign influences. Her polity, then as now, was tribal in character. As a nation, the Japanese possessed the virtues of a tribal community: homogeneity and subordination of the individual to the community; but they also possessed the defects and weaknesses of a primitive community: they revered the tribal sanctions and feared change. They had relentlessly suppressed any attempt to apply reason to the persistent problems of man, the understanding of them and the effort to resolve them constituting his chief warrant for claim to superiority over other animals.

The position in the Western Pacific during the early 1850's was one which the Japanese were studying with great uneasiness. The activities in the north by Russia gave progressively persistent notice of the restlessness of a vigorous continental people and of their gradual but inexorable movement southward along the eastern littoral of Asia. British influence, on the other hand, was steadily being extended northward from Malaya and along the China coast, with indications that the British were giving profound attention to the economic potentialities of Japan as well as of China. European influences, which were fated shortly to conflict with each other, appeared to be moving toward each other along the coast of Asia; conceivably they might meet in Japan, which might well become an arena for the quarrels of European powers.

Although the American Government was cognizant of the trend of these movements in the Pacific, its purpose in sending Commodore Perry to Japan in 1853 was primarily to ameliorate conditions which grew out of the growing commerce of the United States with China and the presence of a large number of American whaling ships off the coast of Japan. The advent in the China trade of steamships, with their limited capacity to carry coal, created insistent need for at least one coaling station intermediate between the Pacific coast of America and China. Further, American vessels had been shipwrecked in Japanese waters, and American seamen, it will be recalled, had been treated with inconceivable brutality. A third consideration was the need for establishing depots in Japan from which American whaling ships could restock themselves and thus obviate

73

the need to make the long haul to Honolulu and back whenever they ran short of supplies.

After incredible obstacles and difficulties, Commodore Perry succeeded on March 31, 1854, in concluding with the Japanese a treaty which, although limited in scope, met the immediate needs of the moment. However, it contained one feature the importance of which the Japanese had not foreseen, and that was the assent of the Japanese to the stationing in Japan of an American consular officer. It was in the exercise of that treaty provision that the United States dispatched to Japan in 1856 its first diplomatic representative, Townsend Harris.

The selection of Harris for the post was an extraordinarily happy one. He had spent many years in the Orient as a merchant; he had acquired a familiar knowledge of Japan and of the Japanese, of their form of government, of their customs, and of their characteristics; and he had dedicated himself to the task of helping the Japanese to prevent the extension to Japan of exploitative practices pursued by the white man in his dealings with the backward peoples of the East. Harris also was keenly aware of the possibility of Japan's becoming a battleground for competitive European influences. So long as Japan remained in seclusion, with her doors shut to foreign intercourse of any kind, she was not entitled to the privileges which membership in the family of nations would confer; and it was Harris' aim to induct Japan into the family of nations under the most favorable auspices. He prepared and, after intolerable delays and indignities imposed upon him by the Japanese, presented to the Japanese Government a Treaty of Commerce and Navigation of the most liberal character possible. He told the Japanese that, this being their first treaty of commerce and navigation, they would be well advised to accept it as he had prepared it, so that when other nations sought special privileges in

74

Japan it would be in order for the Japanese to say to such nations that what was good enough for the United States was good enough for them. It took Harris two years of patient and tactful negotiation before his treaty was signed. But this American did far more than negotiate a treaty. He educated the Japanese officials in the ways of diplomacy, international law, economics, and commerce. He provided Japan with the information which she needed to merge into the world. He answered innumerable questions on every conceivable subject: on social customs of the Occident, mechanics, contemporary science. He taught the principles of currency and exchange. A Japanese, Dr. Inazo Nitobe, wrote of him: "A man of stern rectitude and gentlest powers of persuasion, he, indeed, more than any other, deserves the epithet of benefactor: because in all his dealings with us, the weaker party, he never took advantage of our ignorance, but formulated a treaty with the strictest sense of justice."

I have mentioned at some length America's first representatives to Japan because, in what I shall have to say about Japan's conduct as an international power responsible to the laws of nations, it might otherwise appear that the United States, as the Government responsible for the opening of Japan to the world, had somehow failed to exemplify the conduct we expect in the field of international relations. We can look with pride upon a record of rectitude and honest dealing and the absence of imperialistic design.*

Now what about Japan's own record in the field of international relations? How has she reciprocated the treatment she has received at our hands ever since the time of Townsend Harris?

Let us look at the record.

* The foregoing is based upon material in the manuscript of a book in preparation by a member of my staff at the former American Embassy in Tokyo.

First take the case of Korea. Thirteen hundred and more years ago the Japanese lost a long-held dominion which they possessed at the tip of Korea. The formidable fleets and armies of a resurgent China drove Japan, with Korean help, out of the peninsula; and from the seventh century after Christ to the sixteenth, the Japanese minded the lesson they had been taught by force. At the end of the sixteenth century, the Japanese military dictator, Hideyoshi, launched a grandiose attack on Korea. He himself declared this to be the first step in the conquest of Asia, and he sent insulting letters to the Ming court of China and to the Spanish authorities in the Philippines. He announced that with his forces he would roll China up like a mat and would ultimately proceed against India. But the Chinese Throne sent armies to Korea to help the Koreans; the Japanese, after committing fearful depredations, were stopped; and the imperial ambitions of Japan proved unavailing before the popular resistance of the Koreans and the limitless patience of the Chinese Army.

After the reopening of Japan by Perry, ambitions of Japan on the continent, which had been dormant since the time of Hideyoshi, began again to assert themselves. China maintained over Korea a shadowy suzerainty, which had little significance beyond the tribute paid periodically by the King of Korea to the Emperor of China. That suzerainty was more a manifestation of the cultural sentimentalities between the two countries than it was a definitive political relationship. The Japanese strove, wholly against the wishes of the Koreans, to break that bond. They provoked incidents. They went to war against China in 1894 and 1895, and wrung from a defeated China the solemn recognition of Korean independence.

Nevertheless, the Japanese turned—in the midst of the war with Russia —and thrust upon Korea the status of a dependency. Japan took over

Korea as a protectorate, while renewing her pledges of limited independence for Korea.

Japan demanded independence for Korea; when independence came,
Japan violated it. Japan imposed a protectorate, and promised Korea autonomy. In 1908 the honored and famous Marquis Ito reiterated his Government's pledge by announcing that Japan would not annex Korea. In
1910 Korea was annexed. There are the pledges, and there is the performance.

Another case, the Washington Conference and the years that followed.
In 1921 the representatives of nine governments met in Washington to
consider the problems of the Pacific area and to forge instruments which
would guarantee peace and stability in the Far East. One of the results of
this conference was the Four-Power Treaty, by which four governments—
Japan, the British Empire, France, and the United States—pledged themselves to respect each other's island possessions in the Pacific.

But in 1939 Japan declared without conference with the other con-
tracting parties that she had annexed Spratly Island in the China Sea—an
island that had long been claimed by France. By 1940 it became apparent
from the statements of the Japanese Foreign Minister, Mr. Matsuoka,
that Japan considered any and all islands in the "Greater East Asia"
sphere to be fair game. History has demonstrated only too clearly the
scope of Japan's intentions and the thoroughness of its disregard for its
own pledges.

Japan gave another pledge at the Washington Conference—a pledge
regarding naval limitations. Associating itself with other leading naval
powers who were anxious to bring stability to the Pacific, the Japanese
Government promised to co-operate in reducing the heavy burden of
naval expenditures.

This treaty Japan denounced in 1934, with the result that it expired two years later. While Japan was acting strictly within its legal rights, any hope for stability in the Pacific collapsed with the end of this treaty. Reports of Japan's heavy naval-construction program forced the other naval powers to resume competitive arming, thus fortifying the groundwork for a war in the Pacific.

Look next at Japan's record with regard to the mandated islands in the Pacific. When in 1920 Japan received the mandate for those islands formerly under the German flag, it was with the promise that "no military or naval bases shall be established or fortifications erected in the territory." A further agreement with the United States in 1922 stipulated that American missionaries would be allowed to settle in the islands and that the usual facilities would be extended to American vessels calling at their ports.

And how were these promises honored? From the very beginning Japan discouraged the visits of foreign nationals. Police regulations, delay, every form of obstructionism, were brought to bear on any persons other than Japanese who attempted to enter these islands. When war broke over the Pacific, Japan's lack of faith in holding to her obligations became dangerously apparent.

Pledges were also given to respect the rights of France and the Netherlands to their Pacific possessions.

On February 4, 1922, Japan, along with other countries with interests in the Pacific, informed the Netherlands Government that "it [Japan] is firmly resolved to respect the rights of the Netherlands in relation to their insular possessions in the region of the Pacific Ocean." This pledge was in effect reaffirmed on April 15, 1940, when the Japanese Minister for Foreign Affairs, Mr. Arita, said: "The Japanese Government cannot but be deeply concerned over any development accompanying the aggravation of the war in Europe that may affect the *status quo* of the Dutch East Indies."

As soon, however, as Germany had occupied the Netherlands, Japan used every pressure within her means to extort economic concessions and privileges from the Netherlands East Indies. Nothing but the brave and stubborn resistance of the Netherlands officials to these proposals prevented Japan from forcing the other powers out of this economic market.

On June 19, 1940, the Japanese Foreign Office, through its spokesman, Mr. Suma, announced that the maintenance of the *status quo* in French Indo-China was of equal concern and importance to the Japanese Government.

Yet as soon as French resistance had been broken in Europe, the Japanese Government demanded and obtained special military rights in northern Indo-China. Japanese troops moved into French territory. Airports were taken over. And Japanese officials, true to a form which by now had become pretty well established, went on announcing that their Government had absolutely no designs on territory that was in the very process of being occupied.

Thus, on September 24, 1940, Mr. Suma declared that, far from having any territorial ambitions in French Indo-China, his Government was moving in its armed forces only in order to settle the China affair. This disingenuous remark, which excused one aggression on the claim that it was necessary in order to carry out another, apparently struck Mr. Suma as very good logic.

Again, on December 9, 1940, the Foreign Minister, Mr. Matsuoka, said: "Our objectives in the south are purely economic. We are against conquest, oppression, and exploitation by Japan as much as by any other nation." This, after nearly ten years of armed aggression' in China!

On February 25, 1941, another exhibit was added to this collection of statements when a spokesman for the Japanese military mission in Indo-China insisted that Japan wanted no naval or military bases in southern Indo-China, but only, as he explained, "rubber and rice to help Indo-China prosper in the new order of East Asia." If to take by robbery the commodities of a country means to help that country to "prosper," the lands of the Pacific war under Japanese control are blessed indeed.

But of all the aggressions which have written the name of Japan in infamy upon the pages of history, those against the country and the people of China make the blackest mark. The story goes back a long way, and I can point to but a few of its chapters.

In 1908 Japan and the United States entered into an agreement regarding their respective policies in the Pacific. One of the provisions stated that the two governments "are also determined to preserve the common interest of all powers in China by supporting by all pacific means at their disposal the independence and integrity of China and the principle of equal opportunity for commerce and industry of all nations in that Empire."

Yet in 1915, while most of the great powers were locked in struggle on the European continent, Japan secretly presented to China its notorious "twenty-one demands." You will recall that these demands, if they had been met, would have made of China a vassal state. The terms included recognition of special rights in Shantung, Manchuria, and Mongolia, equal ownership in the largest mining and smelting company in mid-China, leased harbors in Fukien Province, and the employment of none but Japanese advisers. China's Army and Navy were to be trained by Japanese officers, and schools teaching the Japanese language were to be opened throughout the land. No agreements between China and a foreign power with respect to loans, the building of railroads, or the construction of harbors in Fukien were to be made until Japan had been consulted.

By permitting knowledge to be published regarding these demands which Japan had hoped to keep secret, Yuan Shih-kai, President of the young Chinese Republic, was able to obtain a modification of the more flagrant items and a postponement of some of the requests for Japanese control.

In signing the Nine-Power Treaty at Washington, Japan again pledged her respect for China's sovereignty. Specifically, Japan promised to respect "the sovereignty, the independence, and the territorial and administrative integrity of China."

And what was the result of this solemn promise?

In 1931 the military occupation of Manchuria was begun on the flimsiest of pretexts. At the very moment when Japanese armies were overrunning Manchuria, the Japanese Government issued a statement which included the following words: "It may be superfluous to repeat that the Japanese Government harbors no territorial designs in Manchuria." Superfluous indeed! For the world was learning that any such statement was a practical notification of aggressive intent.

In March, 1932, a Japanese puppet regime was installed in Manchuria. This regime shortly afterward signed an agreement which authorized the stationing of large numbers of Japanese troops within its borders. The troops have not been removed to this day.

Eight months after this step had been taken, Mr. Matsuoka, as a delegate, stated before the Council of the League of Nations: "The policy, the hope, the determination of my country, is the maintenance of peace. We want war with no nation. We want no more territory. We are not aggressors. We desire deeply and earnestly the welfare of our great neighbor."

Within a month of Mr. Matsuoka's reassuring statement, Japanese forces had overrun the whole of Manchuria. In 1933 they moved into the adjacent province of Jehol.

Two years later a movement for what was called autonomy in North China was begun by the Japanese. In 1937 war broke out again near Peking. Twenty days after the first exchange of shots near the Marco Polo Bridge, Prince Konoye, then Premier, said: "In sending troops to North China, of course, the Government has no other purpose, as was explained in its recent statement, than to preserve the peace of East Asia."

The peace of East Asia? China has experienced this kind of peace for eleven years. It has suffered the embrace of a self-styled friend who has bombed its civilian population and its undefended cities, wantonly destroyed or expropriated the cherished personal possessions of millions of its people, pursued and machine-gunned the homeless, and committed the atrocities of Nanking paralleled on smaller scale in a thousand and one other places. China knows that what Japan means by peace is utter submission or extinction. China knows what all of us must learn, and learn quickly—that, faced with such a foe, there is no effective argument but crushing, total military defeat of the enemy, and the thorough elimination of the militarist attitude, the militarist training, the militarist institutions, and the militarist leaders who have let loose this plague of destruction.

In 1939 Japan continued her well-made schedule of conquest by occupying the large Chinese island of Hainan and establishing a naval base there. This island, as we now know, was later used as a training base for the troops that were being schooled in the jungle tactics that Japan's militarists were already developing for their attacks in the Philippines, in Malaya, and in Java and throughout the Far East.

In 1940 the now familiar pattern of the Japanese puppet state was imposed upon the provinces of North China, Nanking was dubbed the capital of the renegade "central government" of Wang Ching-wei, and the world was scarcely surprised or startled when Japan recognized this regime as the "National Government of China."

If the world still hoped that after setting up a puppet regime in Manchuria, Japan would at least respect the promises of free commercial opportunity which she had made in the Nine-Power Treaty, it did not have to wait long for disillusionment.

Yet the same sweet words preceded in the usual fashion Japan's shutting of the door. The puppet regime in announcing its independence was made to say: "The foreign policy of the new state shall be to seek and further promote cordial relations with foreign powers by winning their faith and respect, and strictly to observe international conventions. Foreign investments by any nation shall be welcomed for the furtherance of trade and the exploitation of natural resources, thus bringing the principles of the Open Door and equal opportunity and the like to a fuller realization." The so-called protocol by which Japan recognized its puppet state made a point of referring to this pledge.

Yet, as quickly as these promises were made, monopolies in favor of Japanese nationals and corporations were set up which effectively shut out not only American and other Western powers from trading rights, but also the Chinese themselves. And as Japan's military control extended southward in China, American and other non-Japanese business activities were systematically pinched, crowded, or shouldered out. The door to China was to open only at the magic touch of a Japanese. One is reminded of the words with which Perry was greeted: "The place is not designed to treat of anything from foreigners. You will leave here."

There are many other chapters in the story of Japan's pledges and performances—the pledge, for instance, which followed the sinking by the Japanese of the U.S.S. *Panay* and three other American vessels in the Yangtze River. Part of the settlement asked by the United States Government and given by Japan was the assurance that American nationals and property in China would not again be attacked or interfered with. In a note to the United States Government of December 24, 1937, the Japanese Government said, "Rigid orders have been issued to the Military, Naval, and Foreign Office authorities to pay, in the light of the present untoward incident, greater attention than hitherto to observance of the instructions that have been repeatedly given against infringement of, or unwarranted interference with, the rights and interests of the United States and other third powers."

Nevertheless, Japanese forces continued to bomb American property in China. Several hundred of these inexcusable violations are on record in the Department of State.

It is needless to prolong the story through all its chapters. An editor of *The Atlantic Monthly* is credited with the comment, when charged by an aspiring author with having failed to read his whole manuscript, that it is unnecessary to eat a whole egg in order to know that it is bad. It is unnecessary to produce the whole history of Japan's depredations and broken promises. Japan's opening of hostilities without warning, its bombing of open towns—both acts in violation of a convention signed by her Government—would lead us to no different conclusion from that to which the examples already given inevitably and conclusively lead.

Someday another American will land on Japan's shores. He too will come to a country whose government is tottering—perhaps fallen completely. He will come to a land which has tried the way of conquest and found, as other conquerors have found, that the goal was an illusion. He will find a people broken with the burdens of a desperate war—a people hungry, decimated, disillusioned. He will have a great opportunity—he and the other men of the United Nations whose task it will be to bring order out of the chaos of defeat—to take advantage of that disillusionment and to work in co-operation with those within the country who have waited, and even now wait, for such an opportunity.

11

Building the Future—A Postscript

IN THE previous pages I have tried to present the difficult problem our country faces in the Japanese military machine. I have indicated the surprise and the shock I experienced on returning to the United States to find how little the American people as a whole appreciate the dangers we face in fighting this machine, a machine which without any shadow of doubt firmly intends, after consolidating the areas it has temporarily occupied in Greater East Asia, to attack countries in the Western Hemisphere. Only when the American people as a whole fully and clearly recognize this danger and devote themselves to the utmost to the war effort, cheerfully making the sacrifices necessary for that effort, will our country be sure of eventual victory against that enemy.

But victory in itself is not enough. First we must utterly crush, discredit in the eyes of its own people, and render impotent for the future the Japanese military machine and all of its political ramifications. Then, and only then, can we expect to have peace and to build a new world on solid foundations. In that building we must profit by the costly mistakes and shortsightedness that rendered the peace of Versailles so ephemeral. Those errors must never be repeated.

After we have defeated the Axis states, the ghosts of totalitarianism will stalk through the world with prejudice and hate. We can exorcise these ghosts and destroy them if we do not try to meet hate with hate. We must meet hate with cold but sane resolution. We must meet malice, not with malice, but with fine good sense.

Russians, Chinese, Americans, and Japanese will always look out upon the Pacific, and until Providence is pleased to transform the human race to a more complete unity, or to draw the curtain on the drama of mankind, our languages, our cultures, our states remain. Japan cannot be eliminated from this group of peoples. The Japanese people cannot be exterminated, no matter how extreme was the folly of their leaders. The Japanese people must achieve the freedom of civilized men and must take their role in the comity of nations.

That role will be far different from the infantile arrogance of the so-called Greater East Asia Co-Prosperity Sphere. China is and always has been the largest nation, and the fount of culture, in the entire Far East; but there is room, and room to spare, for the people and the culture of Japan. Do you think that I could have fought against war for years, fought it wholeheartedly, if I did not realize that the Japanese were not merely formidable soldiers but were also a people with many sound qualities? I wanted no tradition of hatred to be established between our peoples. Indeed, I could not help see that Japanese-American friendship—however tenuous it might be—was a heritage worth preserving.

We must and shall face the problems of the peace with a broader understanding of the world we live in, knowing that to solve these problems (in the words of Salvador de Madariaga) "our eyes must be idealistic and our feet realistic. We must walk in the right direction but we must walk step by step. Our tasks are: to define what is desirable; to define what is possible at any time within the scheme of what is desirable; to carry out what is possible in the spirit of what is desirable." On these tasks our Government is working with foresight and determination today.

Since my return from Tokyo I have traveled the length and breadth of this land, and I have looked into the faces of tens of thousands of my fellow Americans. They are faces alive with a quiet strength, a sober resolve. They are the faces of men and women who have heard a grim challenge, who are responding to demands which that challenge imposes, and who are looking beyond the horizon. To these men and women, I believe, victory is not only an end, but a beginning. For they are the spiritual descendants of Abraham Lincoln, who said: "The dogmas of the quiet past are inadequate to the stormy present. The occasion is piled high with difficulty, and we must rise with the occasion. As our case is new so we must think anew and act anew."

ABOUT THE AUTHOR

JOSEPH CLARK GREW *served as American Ambassador to Japan from February, 1932, until the attack on Pearl Harbor. He was born in Boston, Massachusetts, in 1880, attended Groton and Harvard, graduating two years before President Roosevelt. After traveling in Europe and the East he was made clerk to the American Consul General at Cairo in 1904. Since then he has made diplomacy his lifework. Before the last war he served in Mexico, Russia, Austria-Hungary, and Germany. He was Counselor to our Embassy in Berlin during the last war and Chargé d'Affaires at Vienna in 1917 when the break came. In 1918 he became acting head of the Western European division of the State Department. He took part in the peace negotiations at Paris and also represented the United States during the negotiations with Turkey at Lausanne in 1922. He has served as Minister to Denmark and to Switzerland and as Ambassador to Turkey. From Turkey he went to Japan. Mr. Grew is married and is the father of three daughters. He is now special assistant to the Secretary of State.*